PENGUIN

GERALDENE H

Geraldene Holt trained as a potte   a teacher. Married to the noted educationist   it, she and her family live in a sixteenth-century thatched farmhouse in Devon.

Cake Stall was written as a result of running a market stall in Tiverton selling cakes, biscuits, cookies and scones using recipes that were tried and tested during twenty years of family cooking and entertaining. Now a well-known food writer, Geraldene Holt contributes to newspapers and magazines and broadcasts regularly on radio and television in the southwest.

Her other books include *Travelling Food*, a culinary guide to picnics, packed lunches and away-day food, and the *Devon Air Cookbook*.

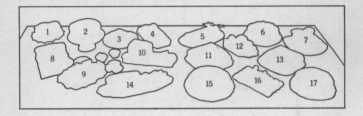

Key to Cover Photograph

1. Date Cake 2. Fat-less Sponge Cake filled with Whipped Cream 3. Smilers, Cinnamon Cookies, Fairy Rings 4. Chocolate Cup Cakes, Coconut Macaroons, Chocolate Eclairs 5. Bûche de Noël 6. Maraschino Cherry Cake 7. Palmiers 8. Chocolate Coconut Cake 9. Iced Gingerbread 10. Date and Walnut Cake 11. Pineapple Upside-Down Cake 12. Queen Cakes 13. Apricot and Almond Cake 14. Cherry Cake 15. Festive Ring 16. Brandy Snaps 17. All-in-one Favourite Chocolate Sponge Cake

GERALDENE HOLT'S CAKE STALL

PENGUIN BOOKS

For my mother, with love

Penguin Books Ltd, Harmondsworth, Middlesex, England
Penguin Books, 40 West 23rd Street, New York, New York 10010, U.S.A.
Penguin Books Australia Ltd, Ringwood, Victoria, Australia
Penguin Books Canada Ltd, 2801 John Street, Markham, Ontario, Canada L3R 1B4
Penguin Books (N.Z.) Ltd, 182–190 Wairau Road, Auckland 10, New Zealand

First published by Hodder & Stoughton 1980
Published in Penguin Books 1983

Reproduced, printed and bound in Great Britain by
Hazell Watson & Viney Limited,
Member of the BPCC Group,
Aylesbury, Bucks

CONTENTS

5

BISCUITS AND COOKIES

INTRODUCTION

It was a bright summer morning as I set off along the narrow Devon lanes to the market. My small car was piled high with delicious fare: sugar-crusted cherry cakes glinted in the sunlight, golden-topped scones shone through their cellophane wrapping. Fruit cakes and chocolate layer cakes sat snug in their boxes, giving that unmistakable aroma of home baking.

I was on my way to my first market. I didn't realise what an exciting enterprise I had embarked upon.

This book is the result of that idea. So many people have requested my recipes that I have collected together the ones that I have found to be most popular at the stall, and added some of my own family favourites. I hope readers will enjoy following the recipes and eating the results. Most of these recipes are not expensive to make, and all are good, healthy family fare. I use butter sparingly; I prefer soft margarine in most cases.

I have given the ingredients in imperial and metric measures, and you can write in the margin your own figures — perhaps in a different colour — if you want to make double or treble the amount. It is important to know how to store cakes, and recommendations for freezer storage are also included. These can be particularly helpful at times like Christmas and the school holidays.

Finally, there is a chapter to help you get good results every time. It tells you about equipment and ingredients for baking, gives you some useful short-cuts to success, and if you feel like selling your cakes, it tells you how to go about it.

Geraldene Holt
August 1980

EQUIVALENCE TABLES

Ounces	Grams	Grams	Ounces
$\frac{1}{4}$	8	1000	2 lb 3 oz
$\frac{1}{2}$	15	500	1 lb 1$\frac{1}{2}$ oz
1	30	250	9
1$\frac{1}{2}$	45	125	4$\frac{1}{4}$
2	55	100	3$\frac{1}{2}$
2$\frac{1}{2}$	70	30	1
3	85		
3$\frac{1}{2}$	100		
4	115		
4$\frac{1}{2}$	130		
5	140		
5$\frac{1}{2}$	155		
6	170		
7	200		
8	225		
9	255		
10	290		
11	310		
12	340		
13	370		
14	400		
15	425		
1 lb	450		
1$\frac{1}{2}$ lb	680		
2 lb	900		
3 lb	1350		

NB: 1000 g = 1 kilogramme

VOLUME

	2 fl oz	55 ml
	3 fl oz	75 ml
¼ pint (1 gill)	5 fl oz	150 ml
½ pint	10 fl oz	275 ml
¾ pint	15 fl oz	425 ml
1 pint	20 fl oz	570 ml
1¾ pint	35 fl oz	1 litre

1 millilitre (ml)	1 gram (g)	a few drops
5 ml	5 g	1 pharmaceutical teaspoon
15 ml	15 g	1 pharmaceutical tablespoon
1 centilitre	10 g	1 dessertspoon
¼ litre	250 g	½ pint less 2 tablespoons
½ litre	500 g	¾ pint plus 4½ tablespoons
1 litre	1000 g (1 kg)	1¾ pint (35 fl oz)

LENGTH

Inches	Centimetres
$\frac{1}{8}$	3 mm (millimetres)
$\frac{1}{4}$	$\frac{1}{2}$ (0.5) cm (centimetre)
$\frac{1}{2}$	1
$\frac{3}{4}$	2
1	2.5
$1\frac{1}{4}$	3
$1\frac{1}{2}$	4
$1\frac{3}{4}$	4.5
2	5
$2\frac{1}{2}$	6.5
3	7.5
4	10
5	13
6	15
7	18
8	20
9	23
10	25.5
11	28
12	30

TEMPERATURE

Electricity and Solid Fuel	Gas Mark	Degrees Fahrenheit	Degrees Centigrade
Cool	¼	200	100
Cool	¼	225	110
Cool	¼–½	250	120
Very slow	1	275	140
Slow	2	300	150
Slow	3	325	160
Moderate	4	350	180
Moderate	5	375	190
Moderately hot	6	400	200
Hot	7	425	220
Very hot	8	450	230
Very hot	9	475	250

These conversion tables have been worked out as practical cooking approximations.

NB: Throughout the book, all spoonfuls are level unless otherwise stated.

GERALDENE HOLT'S CAKE STALL

SCONES AND TEA-BREADS

Scones are at their best when fresh from the oven. They are quick and easy to make, so I usually leave making them until just before tea. However, scones do freeze extremely well, so if you have any left over or have baked a double quantity, pop them into a bag or box and then straight into the freezer. A good scone should be soft and flavoursome, with a thin golden crust on top. I find very few people add eggs. I always do and the results are well worth it.

Scones should be baked in a good hot oven on a floured sheet (not a greased one), to allow for expansion of the scone as it cooks. Just before putting the scones in the oven I brush the tops of the scones with a mixture of egg yolk beaten with a little milk. Then they bake to a shiny golden colour. Remove the scones from the baking sheet with a spatula or flexible knife as soon as you can handle them. Eat straight away! They are delicious with home-made strawberry jam and clotted cream.

Tea-breads are a splendid example of home baking. They are almost unobtainable from commercial bakers, yet they are a tasty unyeasted loaf suitable for slicing and serving spread with butter. I bake a very wide selection of tea-breads, from the moist sweet Welsh tea-bread (where the fruit has been soaked in strong tea overnight) to the delicious savoury celery and walnut tea-bread — sliced, and spread with cream or curd cheese, it makes a very good addition to a lunch-box or a quick snack meal. Two slices of any tea-bread, sandwiched with peanut butter, cheese or chocolate spread, make an excellent mid-morning snack for schoolchildren.

Plain Scones

Cooking time: 12–15 minutes
Oven: 220°C, 425°F, Gas Mark 7
A baking sheet, floured
Quantity: About 12 scones

	METRIC	IMPERIAL
Self-raising flour	225 g	8 oz
Soft margarine	55 g	2 oz
Baking powder	1 × 5 ml spoon	1 teaspoon
Caster sugar	45 g	1½ oz
Salt	⅛ × 5 ml spoon	⅛ teaspoon
1 egg, mixed with milk to make	150 ml	¼ pint
Egg yolk and milk for glaze		

Sieve the flour, salt and baking powder into a bowl. Stir in the sugar. Rub in the margarine quite gently until the mixture resembles fine breadcrumbs. Add all the milk and egg mixture, using a knife to mix it in. The dough will be very soft but not sticky. Turn on to a floured surface and knead lightly into a flat, round shape. Sprinkle the surface of the dough with flour, and with a floured rolling-pin gently roll out until the dough is 1 cm (½ in) thick. Dip a 5 cm (2 in) fluted or plain pastry cutter into some flour, and, using a firm downward movement, cut out as many scones as you can from the sheet of dough. Place the scones on the lightly-floured baking sheet. Knead the rest of the dough together again and cut out more rounds. Using a pastry brush, gently brush the tops of the scones with a mixture of egg yolk with a little milk or top of milk. Bake above the centre of a hot oven for 12–15 minutes. When cool enough to handle, gently remove from sheet and cool on a wire rack. The scones can be eaten at once, or frozen.

To freeze: When completely cooled, pack into boxes or bags and place in freezer. They will keep at least 3 months.
To use: Thaw them out in their wrapping for 1–2 hours and then warm through in the oven or under the grill.

Fruit Scones

Cooking time: 15 minutes
Oven: 220°C 425°F, Gas Mark 7
A baking sheet, floured
Quantity: about 12 scones

	METRIC	IMPERIAL
Self-raising flour	225 g	8 oz
Soft margarine	55 g	2 oz
Baking powder	1 × 5 ml spoon	1 teaspoon
Caster sugar	30 g	1 oz
Salt	⅛ × 5 ml spoon	⅛ teaspoon
Sultanas or raisins	55 g	2 oz
1 egg, mixed with milk to make	150 ml	¼ pint
Egg yolk and milk for glaze		

Use the same method as for plain scones. Stir in the fruit just before adding the liquid.

To freeze: When completely cooled, pack into boxes or bags and place in freezer. They will keep at least 3 months.
To use: Thaw them out in their wrapping for 1–2 hours and then warm through in the oven or under the grill.

Wholewheat Oat Scones

This is a country-style scone with a nutty, crumbly texture. I usually make these for my friends from London. I find they keep extremely well for 2–3 days in a lidded plastic box.

Cooking time: 15 minutes
Oven: 220°C, 425°F, Gas Mark 7
A baking sheet, floured
Quantity: about 20 scones

	METRIC	IMPERIAL
Wholewheat flour	170 g	6 oz
Self-raising white flour	170 g	6 oz
Baking powder	3 × 5 ml spoon	3 teaspoons
Ground ginger	1 × 5 ml spoon	1 teaspoon
Salt	½ × 5 ml spoon	½ teaspoon
Soft margarine	85 g	3 oz
Porridge oats	55 g	2 oz
Golden syrup	4 × 15 ml spoons	4 tablespoons
1 egg, beaten with milk to make	200 ml	7 fl oz

Sieve the dry ingredients into a bowl. Stir in the wholewheat flour. Rub in the margarine, as for plain scones. Stir in the oats. Mix the egg, milk and syrup together, putting 1 tablespoon of liquid aside for brushing the tops of the scones before baking. Add the liquid to the dry ingredients, mixing to a smooth dough with a knife. Turn the dough on to a floured board and gently roll until 1 cm (½ in) thick. Either cut into rounds with a 5 cm (2 in) cutter, or cut with a knife into small triangles. Bake on a floured baking sheet for 15 minutes in a hot oven. Remove with a flexible knife, and cool on a wire rack.

To freeze: When completely cooled, pack into boxes or bags and place in freezer. They will keep at least 3 months.
To use: Thaw them out in their wrapping for 1–2 hours and then warm through in the oven or under the grill.

Cheese Scone Ring

This is a tasty variation of cheese scone — the tops of the scones have a toasted cheese crust. Served warm from the oven with a good bowl of soup, it provides a nourishing lunch or supper.

Cooking time: 15–17 minutes
Oven: 220°C, 425°F, Gas Mark 7

A baking sheet, floured
Quantity: two rings

	METRIC	IMPERIAL
Self-raising flour	225 g	8 oz
Baking powder	1 × 5 ml spoon	1 teaspoon
Salt	$\frac{1}{2}$ × 5 ml spoon	$\frac{1}{2}$ teaspoon
A good pinch of onion or celery salt		
Soft margarine	55 g	2 oz
Grated cheddar cheese	85 g	3 oz
1 egg, mixed with milk to make	150 ml	$\frac{1}{4}$ pint
Grated cheese for topping	30 g	1 oz

Variations: omit the seasoning and add $\frac{1}{2}$ teaspoon ($\frac{1}{2}$ × 5 ml spoon) fresh or dried mixed herbs. Sprinkle the top with them too.

Sieve the flour, baking powder, salt and seasoning into a bowl. Rub in the margarine until the mixture resembles fine bread-crumbs. Stir in the grated cheese and mix in the liquid with a knife to make a soft dough. Turn the dough on to a floured board. Gently knead it, and roll it out to 1 cm ($\frac{1}{2}$ in) thick with a floured rolling-pin. Using a 5 cm (2 in) cutter, cut out 14 scones in all. Arrange 7 scones in each ring on the baking sheet, with the sides of the scones touching. Sprinkle the remaining grated cheese on top of the scones. Bake above the centre of a hot oven for 15–17 minutes. When cool enough to handle, gently remove from sheet and cool on a wire rack, or serve on a folded cloth on a plate to accompany soup.

To freeze: Pack each ring separately in bags or boxes.
To use: Thaw in wrapping at room temperature for 1–2 hours, then
  warm through in a moderate oven for 7 minutes.

Scotch Pancakes

A great many Scotch pancakes are thin and rubbery, but this recipe from Florrie in the village gives a pancake that is light and delicious. I often make these when visitors drop in unexpectedly for tea, because they are quick to make and nicest eaten straight away, although they freeze very well. I find my visitors don't mind standing around in the kitchen chatting while I make these on top of the cooker.

Cooking time: about 4–6 minutes each
Hotplate on medium heat
A heavy griddle or frying pan, well-greased
Quantity: 12 pancakes

	METRIC	IMPERIAL
Self-raising flour	115 g	4 oz
Salt	$\frac{1}{4}$ × 5 ml spoon	$\frac{1}{4}$ teaspoon
Butter or margarine	30 g	1 oz
Caster sugar	55 g	2 oz
Milk	5 × 15 ml spoons	5 tablespoons

1 egg

Sieve the flour and salt into a basin. With a knife cut the butter into the flour until it is in very small pieces. Mix in the sugar. Beat the egg and milk together and add to the mixture. Beat well for 1–2 minutes until a stiff batter results. Heat a well-greased griddle or heavy frying pan, but don't have the pan too hot — Scotch pancakes are baked, not fried! Drop tablespoons of the mixture on to the hot surface. Slightly flatten with the back of the spoon and bake each side for about 3 minutes. Store in a cloth in a basket, ready to serve with bramble jelly or honey.

To freeze: Pack them in sixes in small plastic bags.
To use: Allow to thaw in bags for 2–3 hours at room temperature.

Welsh Tea-Cakes

This is another quick-to-make griddle scone. They have fruit and nutmeg in them, and are best served warm with jam or honey.

Cooking time: about 6 minutes each
Hotplate on medium heat
A griddle or heavy-based frying pan, well-greased
Quantity: about 15 tea-cakes

	METRIC	IMPERIAL
Self-raising flour	225 g	8 oz
Salt	½ × 5 ml spoon	½ teaspoon
Grated nutmeg	½ × 5 ml spoon	½ teaspoon
Caster sugar	85 g	3 oz
Sultanas or raisins	85 g	3 oz
Soft margarine or butter	115 g	4 oz
1 large egg (Size 2)		

Sieve the flour and salt into a mixing bowl. Stir in the nutmeg and sugar. With a knife, cut in the margarine or butter until it is in very small pieces. Rub in if necessary. Stir in the fruit and mix to a dough with the beaten egg. Turn on to a floured board and roll out to 5 mm (¼ in) thickness. Using a 6.5 cm (2½ in) plain cutter, cut out as many rounds as you can. Knead up the trimmings, roll them out again and cut more rounds. Lightly grease the griddle or frying pan. Heat it, but don't have it too hot or the scones will burn. Gently put in as many rounds as you can, and after ½ minute, gently shake the griddle or frying pan to make sure the scones will move a little. Cook for 3 minutes, then turn them over and cook the other side for 3 minutes more. The tea-cakes should have golden-brown, crisp crusts and be soft and cooked inside. Serve them warm — I don't put butter on them. You could mix up a honey spread of half honey and half butter, beaten together and served in a little dish.

To freeze: Pack in lidded boxes or bags.
To use: Leave to thaw in container for 2 hours at room temperature.
 Then warm through in the oven.

Joan's Date and Banana Loaf

This recipe comes from a friend of my mother. It's a lovely soft-textured moist tea-bread and very popular with children.

Cooking time: 50–60 minutes
Oven: 180°C, 350°F, Gas Mark 4
A ½ kg (1 lb) loaf tin, well greased

	METRIC	IMPERIAL
Soft margarine	85 g	3 oz
Caster sugar	115 g	4 oz
1 large egg		
Self-raising flour	200 g	7 oz
Salt	¼ × 5 ml spoon	¼ teaspoon
Bicarbonate of soda	¼ × 5 ml spoon	¼ teaspoon
Chopped dates	115 g	4 oz
2 large ripe bananas, mashed		
Chopped walnuts (optional)	55 g	2 oz

Cream the margarine and sugar until light and fluffy. Beat in the egg, and stir in the rest of the ingredients. Spoon the mixture into the loaf tin. Bake in the middle of a moderate oven for 50–60 minutes, until the tea-bread is firm and just shrinking away from the sides of the tin. Leave to cool in the tin for 5 minutes before turning out on a wire tray.

To freeze: Pack in a bag. I often slice the loaf first; then it is easy to remove one or two slices as needed.
To use; Allow to thaw at room temperature for 2–3 hours.

Honey Orange Tea-Bread

I devised this recipe when I kept bees. Honey keeps cakes moist, and really is a wonder-food — it has over 180 different constituents!

Cooking time: 1–1¼ hours, depending on size
Oven: 170°C, 325°F, Gas Mark 3
One 1 kg (2 lb) tin or two ½ kg (1 lb) tins, greased

	METRIC	IMPERIAL
Self-raising flour	285 g	10 oz
Light soft brown sugar	130 g	4½ oz
A pinch of salt		
Soft margarine	115 g	4 oz
Honey	30 g	1 oz
1 egg, beaten		
The grated rind of an orange		
The juice of an orange, mixed		
with milk to make	75 ml	⅛ pint

Or use this quantity of frozen or bottled orange juice, and add 60 g (2 oz) of candied peel

Melt the honey and margarine together in a saucepan over gentle heat. As the mixture cools, add the orange juice, rind and the beaten egg. Sieve the dry ingredients into a bowl, and add the mixture to them, beating well together. Pour into the loaf tins and bake towards the top of the oven for 1–1¼ hours. Leave in the tins for 5 minutes before turning out to cool on a wire rack.

To freeze: Wrap each loaf separately.
To use: Allow to thaw in wrapping at room temperature for 3–4 hours.

Barbados Tea-Bread

This is a delicious dark, sweet tea-bread containing plenty of black treacle (rich in Vitamin B — and one of Gayelord. Hauser's five wonder foods!). I find it always disappears completely at tea-time.

Cooking time: 1¼–1½ hours
Oven: 180°C, 350°F, Gas Mark 4, then turn down
One 1 kg (2 lb) loaf tin or two ½ kg (1 lb) loaf tins, greased

	METRIC	IMPERIAL
Self-raising flour	285 g	10 oz
A pinch of salt		
Mixed spice	¼ × 5 ml spoon	¼ teaspoon
Ground ginger	½ × 5 ml spoon	½ teaspoon
Soft brown sugar	115 g	4 oz
Sultanas	170 g	6 oz
Chopped candied peel	55 g	2 oz
Black treacle	170 g	6 oz
Milk	3–4 × 15 ml spoons	3–4 tablespoons
Bicarbonate of soda	¼ × 5 ml spoon	¼ teaspoon
1 egg, beaten		

Mix all the dry ingredients together in a bowl. Dissolve the bicarbonate of soda in a little milk, and warm the rest of the milk with the treacle in a saucepan. Heat gently, remove from heat, and then add the beaten egg and the bicarbonate solution. Pour the liquid on to the dry ingredients and mix well. Pour into the tins, and bake first for 30 minutes at 180°C (350°F); then for 45–60 minutes (depending on size) at 170°C (325°F or Gas Mark 3). Leave for 10 minutes to cool in the tins before turning out on to a wire rack. Serve sliced, with butter — although it can be eaten plain.

To freeze: Wrap or pack into boxes.
To use: Allow to thaw in wrapping at room temperature for 3–4 hours.

Welsh Tea-Bread

This is my mother's recipe. She drinks vast amounts of very strong tea, and therefore always has one of the main ingredients to hand. But you do need to start the day before, by soaking the fruit in the tea. The final loaf has a most distinctive taste and is often eaten sliced, without butter. I find it keeps remarkably well in a tin, and up to a month in a plastic bag in the fridge.

Cooking time: 60–70 minutes
Oven: 180°C, 350°F, Gas Mark 4
One 1 kg (2 lb) loaf tin, or two ½ kg (1 lb) loaf tins, greased

	METRIC	IMPERIAL
Sultanas	255 g	9 oz
Raisins	255 g	9 oz
Tea	275 ml	½ pint
Caster sugar	115 g	4 oz
Dark soft brown sugar	115 g	4 oz
Self-raising flour	450 g	1 lb
Golden syrup	1 × 15 ml spoon	1 tablespoon
2 eggs, beaten		
Milk	4 × 15 ml spoon	4 tablespoons

Soak the fruit with the sugars in the hot tea and leave overnight. Next day stir into the fruit (which will now have swollen with the tea) the flour, syrup, beaten eggs and milk. Pour the mixture into the tins and bake for 1 hour for the ½ kg (1 lb) size tins, 1¼–1½ hours if you are using the 1 kg (2 lb) tin. Leave in tin for 5 minutes after removing from oven, then turn out on to a wire rack to cool.

To freeze: Wrap separately and place in freezer.
To use: Leave to thaw in wrapping for 3–4 hours at room temperature.

Apple and Date Tea-Bread

This is a trememdously useful recipe for using up windfall apples or frozen apples which have discoloured slightly. The point is that when you cook the apples with the dates, the apples will darken anyway. This tea-bread has a fresh flavour, and because of its high moisture content it is very soft in texture.

Cooking time: 1 hour
Oven: 180°C, 350°F, Gas Mark 4
One 1 kg (2 lb) loaf tin or two ½ kg (1 lb) loaf tins, greased

	METRIC	IMPERIAL
Self-raising flour	225 g	8 oz
Soft dark brown sugar	115 g	4 oz
Margarine	115 g	4 oz
Stoned dates	115 g	4 oz
Cooking apples	225 g	8 oz
2 eggs		

Stew the peeled sliced apples very gently with 2 tablespoons (2 × 15 ml spoon) of water in a covered saucepan. Remove from heat and mash the cooked apples with a potato masher or a fork. Add the chopped dates, and leave the lid on the saucepan for 10 minutes to allow the dates to soften. Then remove the lid, stir well and allow to cool. Meanwhile, cream the margarine and sugar, and then mix in the beaten eggs, flour and apple-date mixture and beat well. Pour into the prepared tin, and bake towards the top of the oven for 1 hour. Leave in tin for 5 minutes before turning out to cool on a wire rack.

To freeze: Wrap separately or pack in a plastic box.
To use: Allow to thaw in wrapping at room temperature for 3–4 hours.

Honey Crunch Tea-Bread

This tea-bread is very quick to make, and has a lovely honey crunch topping. One advantage of using soft margarine is that all the ingredients can be mixed together fast. This is a specially satisfying tea-bread for lunch boxes, because it contains nuts, fruit, wholewheat flour and honey. We always eat this one plain, without butter.

Cooking time: 65 minutes
Oven: 180°C, 350°F, Gas Mark 4
One 1 kg (2 lb) loaf tin or two ½ kg (1 lb) loaf tins, well-greased

	METRIC	IMPERIAL
Wholewheat flour	55 g	2 oz
Self-raising white flour	170 g	6 oz
Dark soft brown sugar	115 g	4 oz
Soft margarine	115 g	4 oz
Sultanas, raisins or mixed fruit	115 g	4 oz
Chopped nuts	55 g	2 oz
Mixed spice	1 × 5 ml spoon	1 teaspoon
A pinch of salt		
2 medium size eating apples, peeled, cored and grated (Golden Delicious is a good variety to use)		
2 eggs, beaten		
Honey	1 × 15 ml spoon	1 tablespoon

Mix all the ingredients, except for the honey and 15 g (½ oz) of the nuts, together in a bowl and beat steadily for up to 2 minutes. (If you have only 1 egg, you can make do by beating this with 4 × 15 ml spoons — 4 tablespoons — of milk.) Pour the mixture into the prepared tins, and bake towards the top of the oven for 1 hour. Remove from the oven, brush the top of the tea-bread with honey, and sprinkle the remaining nuts on top.

Put it back in the oven for 5 minutes. Leave to cool for 10 minutes before turning out on to a wire rack.

To freeze: Wrap separately, whole or in slices, and pack in box.

To use: Leave to thaw at room temperature for 3–4 hours.

Date and Walnut Loaf

I've discovered many times that this is a really useful standby to have in the freezer, or in the freezing compartment of the fridge. Children can make it because it's an all-in-one mix.

Cooking time: 1 hour
Oven: 190°C, 375°F, Gas Mark 5
A ½ kg (1 lb) loaf tin, well-greased

	METRIC	IMPERIAL
Self-raising flour	225 g	8 oz
Dark soft brown sugar	55 g	2 oz
Soft margarine	55 g	2 oz
Baking powder	1 × 5 ml spoon	1 teaspoon
Golden syrup	1 × 15 ml spoon	1 tablespoon
Chopped dates	85 g	3 oz
Chopped walnuts	55 g	2 oz
1 large egg		
Milk	6 × 15 ml spoons	6 tablespoons

Tip everything into a bowl and stir well for 1 minute. Pour the mixture into the prepared tin and bake in the middle of the oven. Leave to cool in the tin for 5 minutes before turning out on to a wire rack.

To freeze: Wrap in plastic or pack in a lidded box.

To use: Leave to thaw in wrapping for 3–4 hours at room temperature.

Celery and Walnut Loaf

This makes an excellent, firmly-crusted tea-bread for a picnic. I serve it spread thickly with home-made curd cheese and covered in chopped herbs from the garden. But you can use any kind of spreading cheese with it.

Cooking time: 1 hour
Oven: 190°C, 375°F, Gas Mark 5
A ½ kg (1 lb) loaf tin, well greased

	METRIC	IMPERIAL
Self-raising white flour	225 g	8 oz
Wholewheat flour	55 g	2 oz
Soft margarine	85 g	3 oz
Chopped walnuts	70 g	2½ oz
2 sticks of celery, chopped		
Salt	1 × 5 ml spoon	1 teaspoon
1 egg		
Milk	150 ml	¼ pint

Rub the margarine into the two flours, with the salt. Stir in the chopped nuts and the celery. Mix to a soft dough with the milk and egg. Knead lightly in the bowl, and shape roughly to fit the tin. Bake towards the top of the oven for 1 hour. Allow to cool for 5 minutes before turning out on to a wire rack.

To freeze: Wrap separately, or pack in a plastic box.
To use: Thaw for 3–4 hours at room temperature.

GERALDENE HOLT'S CAKE STALL

SPONGE CAKES

I find that more people have problems with sponge cakes than with any other kind of cake, so that after one or two failures, many people won't attempt them again. Yet a freshly-baked, light and springy sponge cake, oozing with jam and possibly cream as well, is a fabulous tea-time treat. Lots of people are forced into buying a rather tasteless commercial equivalent, and this seems a great pity. I hope that the instructions in this chapter for making a whole range of sponge cakes will enable you to achieve just what you want, so that you can always rely on being able to produce an excellent cake quite quickly.

The first thing to point out is that there are at least four kinds of sponge cake. The lightest by far is the *Fatless Sponge*, and this is an immensely useful cake. It may look very plain when served with just a jam filling, but it can make a marvellous background for more exciting fillings and icings. And the fatless sponge with a fatless filling is a good cake for people on a strict fat-free diet, and therefore often very popular with older folk.

The second main type of sponge cake is the *Genoese Sponge*. It is just as useful as the fatless sponge, but has the added advantage of keeping longer because of its fat content. I find I prefer the modified Genoese sponge, which contains only half as much fat as the original version. This variation seems to be more reliable, and is very popular with home bakers.

The third type is by far the biggest group — the *Victoria Sponge*. Many people know of no other kind. This is much easier to make, which probably explains its great popularity.

The fourth type is essentially a variant of the *Victoria Sponge*: the ingredients are often identical, but the method is different. This is the *All-in-one-mix Sponge*. This kind is particularly convenient if you have an electric mixer, and it is a good type to start with if you have any worries about baking sponge cakes. And I hope that, flushed with success after attempting these, you will be bold enough to try some of the others. Don't worry if it takes a little practice — rejected sponge cakes are splendid for trifles, or for turning into a super orange fool (see page 234).

34

Whisked Fatless Sponge Cake

This is an excellent sponge to make for eating when freshly baked, or within the day. The eggs and sugar are first whisked to incorporate a great deal of air in the resulting foam. There are three ways of doing this, if you are making a whisked sponge, by hand:

1 Separate the yolks from the whites. Put the whites into a large bowl and the yolks into a cup. Beat the egg whites until really stiff. Gradually whisk in the sugar. After half the sugar has been added, whisk in the rest of the sugar alternately with the yolks, a spoonful at a time. Then fold in the sieved flour.

2 With this method you need two bowls, and this can be inconvenient at times. Again, separate the egg yolks from the whites. Then in one bowl whisk the egg yolks and sugar until very light, foamy and much increased in volume. In the other bowl, whisk the egg whites until very stiff. (If you have to use the same whisk, this means washing and very thoroughly drying it before you move from the yolks to the whites — all very tedious.) Then fold the beaten egg whites into the beaten yolk and sugar mixture before folding in the flour.

3 This is the most used method, although it takes 15–20 minutes. Select a large bowl that will fit over a saucepan containing 2.5 cm (1 in) of very hot water. Now whisk all the sugar and all the eggs until the mixture is thick, pale and very creamy — until the whisk, when removed from the bowl, leaves a trail across the top of the mixture. Then remove the bowl from the hot steam and gently fold in the sieved flour.

To make a whisked sponge in an electric mixer, you can use Method 3 but without the steam treatment. Make sure, though, that the mixing bowl is pre-warmed.

Cooking time: 20–25 minutes

Oven: 180°C, 350°F, Gas Mark 4
2 × 18–19 cm (7–7½ in) sandwich tins, greased and base-lined

	METRIC	IMPERIAL
4 eggs		
Caster sugar	115 g	4 oz
Plain flour	115 g	4 oz
Filling and topping:		
Raspberry jam	2 heaped 15 ml spoons	2 heaped tablespoons
Whipped cream	150 ml	¼ pint
Caster sugar	2 × 5 ml spoons	2 teaspoons

Make sure all the ingredients are at room temperature — the flour and sugar can be quite warm. Sieve the flour at least twice, and store the sieved flour in a warm place, on a plate or piece of greaseproof paper (this has the advantage that it is easier to shoot the flour back into the sieve). Depending on whether you are whisking by hand or in an electric mixer, select your method of whisking. When the eggs and sugar are whisked, sieve some of the flour on to the egg mixture. Gently fold in with a metal spoon, using a figure-of-eight movement to ensure the retention of air in the mixture. Repeat until all the flour has been incorporated. Pour the mixture into the two prepared tins. Pop each tin on the scales to check that each has exactly half of the mixture. Bake in the centre of a moderate oven for 20–25 minutes, until the cake is golden, well risen and just beginning to shrink from the sides of the tin. Leave to cool in the tin for 1–2 minutes, making sure that the cake is not in a draught from an open door or window. Then turn out to cool on a wire rack.

When the cakes are cool, sandwich them with jam and possibly whipped cream too, if you wish. Sprinkle the top of the cake with sieved caster sugar.

To freeze: Store filled or unfilled in a lidded container.
To use: Thaw in container at room temperature for 3 hours.

Genoese Sponge Cake

I make this modified Genoese sponge when I want a very light sponge which will keep a little longer. I always use Method 3 for this sponge cake.

Cooking time: 25 minutes
Oven: 185°C, 365°F, Gas Mark 4½
2 × 18–19 cm (7–7½ in) sandwich tins, greased and base-lined

	METRIC	IMPERIAL
4 eggs		
Caster sugar	115 g	4 oz
Plain flour	115 g	4 oz
Melted butter or soft margarine	45 g	1½ oz
Filling and topping:		
Jam	4 × 15 ml spoons	4 tablespoons
Whipped cream (optional)	150 ml	¼ pint
Marzipan (optional)	115 ml	4 oz
Caster sugar	2 × 5 ml spoons	2 teaspoons

First sieve the flour twice, and store in a warm place on a piece of cooking paper. Whisk the eggs and sugar together for 10 minutes in an electric mixer, or 15–20 minutes over hot water if using a hand whisk. When the mixture is really foamy, light and creamy and the whisk leaves a trail over the top of the mixture, sieve in some of the flour. Fold in with the electric whisk held in the hand, or with a metal spoon. Now very gently pour in a little melted butter — not too hot — then some flour, and fold in with a figure-of-eight movement. Carefully continue with the flour and butter until they are incorporated, making sure you don't lose too much air from the mixture and reduce its capacity. Pour into the two prepared tins, and bake in the centre of a moderately hot oven for 25 minutes. Leave to cool in the tin for 2 minutes out of the way of any draughts, then turn out and cool

on a wire rack. When cold, sandwich with raspberry jam, or jam
and whipped cream, or a thin layer of jam and a thin layer of
marzipan — this gives a lovely almond flavour. Sprinkle the
cake with sieved caster sugar.

To freeze: Store filled or unfilled in a lidded container. If unfilled,
  separate the layers with greasproof paper.
To use: Thaw in container at room temperature for 3 hours.

Victoria Sponge Cake

When this cake was made in Victorian England, only butter was
used. I think, though, that soft margarine is just as acceptable.
Once again, do make sure you start with all the ingredients at
room temperature, and make sure that you beat in the sugar
and fat until they are really pale and fluffy. This is no problem if
you have an electric mixer.

Cooking time: 30–35 minutes
Oven: 180°C, 350°F, Gas Mark 4
2 × 18 cm (7 in) sandwich tins, greased and base-lined

	METRIC	IMPERIAL
Soft margarine	115 g	4 oz
Caster sugar	115 g	4 oz
2 large eggs		
Vanilla essence	$\frac{1}{2}$ × 5 ml spoon	$\frac{1}{2}$ teaspoon
Self-raising flour	115 g	4 oz
Filling:		
Jam or lemon curd	4 × 15 ml spoons	4 tablespoons

Sieve the flour and store in a warm place. Now, in a warmed
bowl, beat the soft margarine and the sugar with a wooden
spoon until really pale in colour and fluffy looking. (This takes
2–3 minutes in an electric mixer.) Break the eggs into a cup and

38

whisk them with a fork to break them up. Add the vanilla essence and stir. Now gradually add the egg to the light and fluffy mixture in the bowl, a spoonful at a time, beating in well each time. Towards the end you may add a little of the sieved flour each time, too. Now sift a thin layer of flour on to the mixture and gently fold in with a metal tablespoon. Repeat until all the flour has been incorporated. Divide the mixture between the two prepared tins and level the tops. Bake in the centre of a moderate oven for 30–35 minutes, until the cakes are golden brown and feel springy to the touch. Leave the cakes in the tins to cool for 2 minutes, then turn out on to a wire rack. When cook, sandwich with raspberry jam or with a fresh lemon curd, which is very simple to make.

Lemon Curd

	METRIC	IMPERIAL
The finely grated rind and juice of one lemon		
Granulated sugar	85 g	3 oz
Cornflour	$\frac{1}{4}$ × 5 ml spoon	$\frac{1}{4}$ teaspoon
1 egg		
Butter	30 g	1 oz

Simply heat, in a small saucepan, the grated rind and juice of the lemon together with the sugar, cornflour, egg and butter. Stir until the mixture boils then, as soon as it clears and thickens, remove from the heat and cool. Sandwich the cake with the filling and sprinkle the top with sieved caster sugar. The cake is delicious eaten straight away, but a Victoria sponge does freeze extremely well.

To freeze: Store in a lidded container.
To use: Thaw in container at room temperature for 3–4 hours.

All-in-one-mix Victoria Sponge Cake

This is the easiest of all the sponge cakes to make, but because one hasn't spent so long beating air into the mixture, the cake depends upon a little more raising agent in the form of baking powder. The result, though, is a very good cake, and this is certainly the one to start with if you are at all hesitant about making a sponge cake.

Cooking time: 30–35 minutes
Oven: 180°C, 350°F, Gas Mark 4
2 × 18 cm (7 in) sandwich tins, greased and base-lined

	METRIC	IMPERIAL
Soft margarine	115 g	4 oz
Caster sugar	115 g	4 oz
2 large eggs		
Vanilla essence	$\frac{1}{4}$ × 5 ml spoon	$\frac{1}{4}$ teaspoon
Self-raising flour	115 g	4 oz
Baking powder	1 × 5 ml spoon	1 teaspoon
Filling and topping:		
Jam	4 × 15 ml spoons	4 tablespoons
or		
Whipped cream	150 ml	$\frac{1}{4}$ pint
Chopped pineapple or other fruit	2 × 15 ml spoons	2 tablespoons
Caster sugar	2 × 5 ml spoons	2 teaspoons

For this cake, everything must be at room temperature. Sieve the flour and baking powder into a mixing bowl and then add the sugar, soft margarine, eggs and vanilla essence. Beat the mixture together well for 1 minute with either a wooden spoon or an electric beater. Pour the mixture into two tins and level the surface of the cakes. Bake in the centre of a moderate oven for 30–35 minutes, until golden brown and springy to the touch.

Cool in the tins for 1 minute, then turn out and cool on a wire rack.

Sandwich with jam, or whipped cream mixed with chopped fruit: for example, pineapple to which a little sugar has been added. Finally, sprinkle with sieved caster sugar.

To freeze: Store filled or plain in a lidded container. If plain, separate layers with greaseproof paper.
To use: Thaw in container at room temperature for 4 hours.

Coffee Sponge Layer Cake

I've always found this a tremendously popular cake. I use a fatless sponge because the butter cream icing which sandwiches and covers the cake is quite rich.

Cooking time: 25 minutes
Oven: 180°C, 350°F, Gas Mark 4
2 × 18–19 cm (7–7½ in) sandwich tins, greased and base-lined

	METRIC	IMPERIAL
4 eggs		
Caster sugar	115 g	4 oz
Coffee essence	2 × 5 ml spoons	2 teaspoons
Plain flour	115 g	4 oz
Icing:		
Icing sugar	340 g	12 oz
Butter or soft margarine	170 g	6 oz
Coffee essence or powder	1 × 15 ml spoon	1 tablespoon
Hot water	2 × 15 ml spoons	2 tablespoons

Decoration:
8 chocolate drops or 'Matchmaker' sticks

41

Sieve the flour twice on to a piece of greaseproof paper. Whisk the eggs and sugar over hot water — if using a hand whisk, for 15 minutes — until it is pale and foamy and the whisk leaves a trail across the mixture. Remove from the heat and slowly add the coffee essence. Continue whisking for 3 minutes. Gently sift a layer of flour over the mixture, and fold in with a metal spoon. Repeat until all the flour has been added. Pour into the two prepared tins and bake in the centre of a moderate oven for 20–25 minutes, until well risen and springy to the touch. Leave to cool in tin for 1–2 minutes, then turn out on to a wire rack. Make the icing by beating the butter until soft, and then gradually beat in the sieved icing sugar. Mix to a soft icing by adding the coffee blended with the water. Sandwich the cakes with some of the butter cream and spread it over the sides of the cake. Put 2–3 tablespoons of icing into a piping bag and then use the rest of the icing to spread over the top of the cake. Pipe whirls of coffee butter cream around the edge of the cake. Cut the chocolate sticks or buttons in half and place each piece between the whirls, pointing towards the centre. Leave for 1–2 hours to set.

To freeze: This cake freezes well if stored in a lidded container kept upright.
To use: Thaw in container in a cool temperature overnight.

All-in-one Favourite Chocolate Sponge

This is a splendid cake which is always admired and enjoyed. And it is so easy! Do try this recipe if you are worried about producing a good chocolate sponge. It's deliciously dark and moist, with a scrumptious filling and icing. Another big advantage is that you don't need cooking chocolate — the recipe uses cocoa. If you don't wish to make the frosting, this cake is particularly gorgeous filled with whipped cream and covered with melted chocolate.

Cooking time: 30–35 minutes
Oven: 180°C, 350°F, Gas Mark 4
2 × 18 cm (7 in) sandwich tins, or one tin this diameter but 5 cm (2 in)
deep, greased and base-lined

	METRIC	IMPERIAL
Caster sugar	115 g	4 oz
Soft margarine	115 g	4 oz
2 large eggs		
Self-raising flour	115 g	4 oz
Baking powder	1 × 5 ml spoon	1 teaspoon
Cocoa	3 × 15 ml spoons	3 tablespoons
Coffee powder	1 × 5 ml spoon	1 teaspoon
Hot water	3 × 15 ml spoons	3 tablespoons
Chocolate frosting:		
Icing sugar	85 g	3 oz
Cocoa	30 g	1 oz
Caster sugar	55 g	2 oz
Soft margarine	45 g	1½ oz
Water	2 × 15 ml spoons	2 tablespoons

Make sure, first, that all the ingredients are at room temperature.
The sugar and flour can be quite warm.

Mix the cocoa, coffee and hot water together in a cup. Then put
the sieved flour and baking powder, together with the sugar,
soft margarine and eggs, into a bowl. Add the cocoa mixture
and mix everything together, then beat for 1 minute until well
mixed and of a soft consistency. Divide the mixture into the two
tins and bake in the centre of a moderate oven for 30–35
minutes, or for 45 minutes if using one deep tin — until the
cakes are springy to the touch and just shrinking away from the
tin. Leave to cool in the tins for 5 minutes, and then turn out on
to a wire rack. If you have used one tin, cut the cake into two
layers when cool.

Now make the frosting by sieving the icing sugar and cocoa into a bowl. Then in a saucepan gently heat the sugar, margarine and water. Stir until the sugar is dissolved. Allow the mixture to boil and then remove from the heat and pour on to the sieved icing sugar and cocoa. Beat until smooth and runny. This frosting thickens as it cools. When it has cooled a little pour almost half the frosting on to one of the cakes, and put the other cake on top. Pour the rest of the icing over the top of the cake and let it trickle down the sides. Decorate, if you wish, with flaked almonds.

To freeze: It freezes perfectly. Wrap it in plastic, or store in a lidded container.
To use: Thaw in wrapping or container for 3–4 hours at room temperature.

Fudge-Filled Sponge

I find this recipe is ideal when I've run out of icing sugar — it's for a Victoria sponge with fudge filling.

Cooking time: 40–45 minutes
Oven: 180°C, 350°F, Gas Mark 4
An 18 cm (7 in) tin, 6 cm ($2\frac{1}{2}$ in) deep, greased and base-lined

	METRIC	IMPERIAL
Soft margarine	115 g	4 oz
Caster sugar	115 g	4 oz
2 large eggs		
Vanilla essence	$\frac{1}{4}$ × 5 ml spoon	$\frac{1}{4}$ teaspoon
Self-raising flour	115 g	4 oz
Fudge filling:		
Soft light brown sugar	115 g	4 oz
Soft margarine	55 g	2 oz
Coffee essence	1 × 5 ml spoon	1 teaspoon

Golden syrup	1 × 15 ml spoon	1 tablespoon
Milk	1 × 15 ml spoon	1 tablespoon
Topping:		
Icing sugar (optional)	1 × 15 ml spoon	1 tablespoon

Make sure all the ingredients are at room temperature. Then cream the margarine and sugar until really light and fluffy. Beat in the vanilla essence then — gradually — the eggs. Fold in the sieved flour and pour into the prepared cake tin. Bake in the centre of a moderate oven for 40–45 minutes, until the cake is golden and just shrinking away from the sides of the tin. Cool in the tin for 2 minutes, then turn out on a wire rack. When cool, cut into two layers.

To make the fudge filling, measure the ingredients into a small saucepan and gently bring to the boil. Simmer, stirring all the time, for 5 minutes. Remove from heat and allow to cool for a few minutes; beat as the filling cools and thickens. Then sandwich the two halves of the cake with the filling. If you have some, sift icing sugar over the top of the cake, and then make a lattice pattern by drawing the back of a knife over the top.

To freeze: Wrap in plastic, or store in a lidded container.
To use: Thaw in wrapping or container for 3–4 hours at room temperature.

Orange or Lemon Sponge Sandwich

An orange- or lemon-flavoured Victoria sponge sandwich, iced with a honey-orange icing, is always a delight to serve at tea. Customers at the cake stall tell me that this cake freezes really well.

45

Cooking time: 40–45 minutes
Oven: 180°C, 350°F, Gas Mark 4
An 18 cm (7 in) cake tin, 6 cm (2½ in) deep or 2 sandwich tins of this
diameter, greased and base-lined

	METRIC	IMPERIAL
Soft margarine	115 g	4 oz
Caster sugar	115 g	4 oz
The finely grated rind of an orange		
2 large eggs		
Self-raising flour	115 g	4 oz
Icing:		
Icing sugar	170 g	6 oz
Butter or soft margarine	85 g	3 oz
Honey	2 × 5 ml spoons	2 teaspoons

The juice of one orange
2–3 drops orange food colouring
1 drop orange flower water
(optional)
5–6 crystallised orange slices

Cream the sugar and margarine in a bowl (warmed in cold
weather) until light and fluffy. Beat in the grated orange rind and
the eggs, a little at a time. Gently fold in the sieved flour and
pour the mixture into the prepared tin. Bake in the centre of a
moderate oven for 40–45 minutes until golden and just starting
to shrink from the tin. Cool in the tin for 3 minutes before
turning out on to a wire tray. When quite cool, cut into two
layers (unless you have used two separate tins) with a finely
serrated knife using a gentle sawing movement.
Make the icing by beating the butter and honey until soft, then
gradually add the sieved icing sugar and the strained orange
juice. When it is soft and creamy, add the drops of colouring (dip
a skewer into the bottle and use as a dropper), to give a pale,
delicate orange shade, and add the orange flower water. Use
this to sandwich the cake layers, and spread the top with the rest

of the icing. Make a swirling pattern with the end of a knife and decorate with the orange slices, cut into halves.

The lemon version is made in just the same way, but use a lemon instead of the orange, yellow instead of the orange colouring, and crystallised lemon slices.

To freeze: Store in a lidded container.
To use: Thaw in container in a cool place overnight.

Swiss Roll

Swiss rolls never fail to disappear from the tea-table or cake stall. Try this one sandwiched with home-made jam or jelly, possibly with a layer of whipped cream included as well. For a coffee swiss roll, add 2 teaspoons of coffee essence to the mixture and fill with a cinnamon butter cream. To make a chocolate swiss roll, use the recipe for Bûche de Noël.

Cooking time: about 12–15 minutes
Oven: 200°C, 400°F, Gas Mark 6
A swiss roll tin, about 30 cm × 20 cm (12 in × 8 in); use greaseproof paper on the base and at each end, and grease the tin and paper well

	METRIC	IMPERIAL
Caster sugar	55 g	2 oz
2 large eggs		
Plain flour	55 g	2 oz
A pinch of baking powder		
Warm water	1 × 15 ml spoon	1 tablespoon
Filling and topping:		
Jam or jelly	5 × 15 ml spoons	5 tablespoons
Caster sugar	2 × 15 ml spoons	2 tablespoons

47

Sieve the flour twice on to a piece of greaseproof paper, and store in a warm place. Whisk the eggs and sugar in a bowl over hot water until the mixture is pale and creamy, and the whisk leaves a trail over the surface. Gently fold in the sieved flour and the warm water, and pour into the swiss roll tin. Spread the mixture evenly, and bake in a moderately hot oven for 12 minutes, until the cake is springy to the touch in the centre. While the cake is cooking, prepare a piece of greaseproof paper a little larger than the tin, by sprinkling it with caster sugar. If your jam for the filling is stiff, warm it in a saucepan. When the roll is baked, take it from the oven and turn it straight on to the sugared paper. Peel off the lining paper and with a sharp knife trim the crusty edges. Spread the warmed jam over the roll and then gently lift the shorter side of the roll, fold it over for about 1 cm ($\frac{1}{2}$ in) and start rolling. Raise the paper underneath as you do this and continue to roll the cake, using the paper to help it along. When completely rolled up, leave the paper around it for 1–2 minutes, then remove and put the swiss roll to cool on a wire rack, with its end tucked underneath. Dust with sieved caster sugar.

To freeze: When completely cool, store in a lidded container.
To use: Thaw in container at room temperature for 3–4 hours.

Sponge Flan

I am always shocked to see how expensive these are in the shops. Yet once you've acquired a non-stick flan tin they become very easy to make. Flan cases are excellent for storing in the freezer, because they defrost so quickly. On one occasion I tipped hot stewed fruit into a frozen one, decorated it with whipped cream and served it within 5 minutes! I also like chocolate flan cases filled with coffee mousse or, for children, with a lime-flavoured milk jelly sprinkled with crumbled choco-late flake. A coffee sponge flan filled with a compote of sliced oranges in caramel syrup makes another first-rate pudding.

Any of the sponge mixtures can be used for a sponge flan. I prefer the fatless sponge, because it is very light, and one can then indulge in a whipped cream decoration.

Cooking time: 10–15 minutes
Oven: 180°C, 350°F, Gas Mark 4
A 19 cm (7½ in) non-stick flan tin, greased

	METRIC	IMPERIAL
Caster sugar	55 g	2 oz
2 large eggs		
Plain flour	55 g	2 oz
A pinch of baking powder		
Filling:		
Strawberries, raspberries, or other fruit	340 g	12 oz
Caster sugar	2 × 15 ml spoons	2 tablespoons
Whipped cream	150 ml	¼ pint
Arrowroot or gelatine	½ × 5 ml spoon	½ teaspoon

Sift the flour and baking powder twice on to a piece of paper. Store in a warm place. Whisk the sugar and eggs together in a bowl over hot water until the whisk leaves a trail across the mixture. Remove from heat, whisk for 2 minutes more, then sift some flour on to the mixture and fold in with a metal spoon. Repeat sifting and folding until all the flour has been added. Pour into a well-greased flan tin. Bake in the centre of a moder-ate oven for 10–15 minutes, until the sponge is golden and springy to the touch. Cool in tin for 2 minutes. Then gently slip a knife between the cake and the tin around the edge, and turn out on to a wire rack.

To fill:

Hull the strawberries and rinse quickly with water. Leave in a bowl sprinkled with the caster sugar for at least 30 minutes. Then gently pour off the fruit syrup into a small saucepan. To make a thickened glaze, cook the syrup with the arrowroot until it is clear. Allow to cool a little. Arrange the strawberries in the flan case and spoon the glaze over them. To make a set glaze (which is nicer in hot weather), gently heat the fruit syrup with the gelatine until it is dissolved. Cool the glaze until it has started to set before spooning over the fruit in the flan. Complete by spooning or piping the whipped cream around the edge of the flan.

To freeze: I prefer to freeze flan cases unfilled, wrapped in plastic.
To use: Thaw in wrapping at room temperature for 1 hour.

Austrian Coffee Cake

This is a delicious rum-and-coffee-soaked sponge cake, masked with whipped cream and decorated with toasted almonds. For a buffet party, I make this cake in a ring tin; but it is just as attractive baked in a round-based pudding basin.

Cooking time: 40–45 minutes
Oven: 190°C, 375°F, Gas Mark 5
An 18–20 cm (7–8 in) ring cake tin, or a 1 litre (2 pint) pudding basin, well-greased

	METRIC	IMPERIAL
Soft margarine	170 g	6 oz
Caster sugar	170 g	6 oz
3 eggs		
Self-raising flour	170 g	6 oz
Strong black coffee	275 ml	½ pint

Rum or brandy	75 ml	small wine glass
Double cream	275 ml	½ pint
1–2 drops vanilla essence		
Caster sugar	1 × 15 ml spoon	1 tablespoon
Toasted flaked almonds	30 g	1 oz

In a warmed bowl cream the margarine and sugar until light and fluffy. Gradually beat in the eggs, and then fold in the sieved flour. Spoon into the cake tin or bowl. Level the top of the mixture. Bake in the centre of a moderately hot oven for 40–45 minutes, until golden and springy to the touch. Leave in the tin for 4 minutes before turning on to a wire tray to cool. Now pour the rum or brandy into the coffee and sweeten to taste. Replace the cake in the tin when cool, and soak the cake with the coffee-rum mixture. Gradually it will all be soaked up. Then whip the cream, and flavour it with the vanilla essence and a very little sugar, or use vanilla sugar. Turn the cake on to a platter and spread or pipe the whipped cream all over the cake. Decorate with the toasted almonds.

To freeze: Freeze the cake before soaking with coffee mixture.
To use: Thaw in container for 2–3 hours then soak with coffee mixture and decorate.

Tipsy Cake

This is a tempting chocolate sponge cake soaked in sherry and topped with a thick layer of very light cream. For a dinner party I make it in a brioche tin or a ring cake tin, which looks very attractive.

Cooking time: 30–35 minutes
Oven: 180°C, 350°F, Gas Mark 4
A 19–20 cm (7½–8 in) round cake tin, greased and base-lined

	METRIC	IMPERIAL
Caster sugar	115 g	4 oz
Soft margarine	115 g	4 oz
2 large eggs		
Self-raising flour	115 g	4 oz
Baking powder	1 × 5 ml spoon	1 teaspoon
Cocoa	3 × 15 ml spoons	3 tablespoons
Strong coffee	3 × 15 ml spoons	3 tablespoons
A small wine glass of sherry		
Double cream	150 ml	¼ pint
1 egg white		
Caster sugar	2 × 5 ml spoons	2 teaspoons

In a warm bowl, mix the cocoa with the coffee, and sift in the flour and the baking powder. Add the sugar, margarine and eggs, and beat all together for at least 1 minute. Pour into the greased and lined tin and bake in the centre of a moderate oven for 30–35 minutes, until the cake is springy to the touch and just starting to shrink away from the tin. Cool in tin for 2 minutes, then turn on to a wire rack. When cool, put the cake on a serving plate with a slight rim and soak it well with the sherry. Now whip the egg white until stiff. Gradually add the sugar and whisk again. Whip the double cream and when stiff but still glossy, fold in the beaten egg white. Pile on to the sherry-soaked cake and swirl into peaks. Sprinkle the top with a little cinnamon mixed with caster sugar or grated chocolate. Store in a cool place for at least 1 hour before serving.

To freeze: Take the plain unsoaked cake and wrap it or store it in a lidded container.
To use: Thaw in container at room temperature for 3–4 hours. Then soak in sherry and top with cream.

Strawberry Party Gâteau

This is a quickly prepared rectangular sponge-based gâteau. Any fruit, fresh or frozen, can be used; fresh strawberries always work well but apricots, raspberries, pears or peaches would all be tempting. Because the cake is oblong, it slices well and economically for a party.

Cooking time: 25 minutes
Oven: 180°C, 350°F, Gas Mark 4
A 28 cm × 18 cm × 2.5 cm (11 in × 7 in × 1 in) baking tin, greased and base-lined

	METRIC	IMPERIAL
Caster sugar	55 g	2 oz
2 eggs		
Plain flour	55 g	2 oz
Butter (melted)	15 g	½ oz
Filling and topping:		
Strawberries	225 g	½ lb
Double cream	275 ml	½ pint
Vanilla sugar	1 × 15 ml spoon	1 tablespoon
Some ratafias or chopped nuts		

Twice sieve the flour, and store on a piece of paper in a warm place. Whisk the eggs and sugar until really light and foamy — do this over warm water if using a hand whisk. Gently fold in the flour and melted butter. Pour into the prepared tin and bake in the centre of a moderately hot oven for 20–25 minutes. Leave to cool in the tin for 1 minute before turning out on to a wire rack. Hull the strawberries and rinse them if necessary. Reserve half — the best ones — for the top of the cake. Cut the rest into halves and sprinkle with sugar. Whip the cream with a little vanilla sugar, and put about a third of the cream into a piping bag. With a finely serrated knife, cut the sponge cake in half, lengthwise. Spread the lower half with half the remaining cream, distribute the cut strawberries on the cream, and then lower the top half on to the filling. Spread a thin layer of cream on the top of the gâteau and use the rest to cover the sides. Press crushed ratafias or nuts on to the sides. Arrange the whole strawberries on the top. Pipe cream around the rim of the top and around the base. Set aside to mature for at least 1 hour — longer, if you have time.

To freeze: Store the unfilled sponge cake in a bag or container.
To use: Thaw at room temperature in container for 1 hour, then assemble.

GERALDENE HOLT'S
CAKE STALL

TEA-TIME AND
FAMILY CAKES

These are the cakes that home baking is all about, the cakes that always give pleasure, the cakes I am always happy to put on the table. There's no other way of obtaining these cakes — the commercial bakeries couldn't contemplate producing such a wide range. And, of course, these cakes have the real taste of home baking locked into them. I'm sure you'll be delighted with the results from any of these recipes; I've made all of them hundreds of times, and they never fail.

Cherry Cake

There is something wonderfully timeless about cherry cake. I really have to restrain myself from cutting a slice while it cools on a wire rack. Most cakes taste excellent while still warm, but they don't go anything like as far that way. So try to wait until everyone is home for tea before serving them with sugar-crusted cherry cake, preferably on a rectangular plate. This is the recipe I worked out for the cake stall, and I find it first-rate.

Cooking time: 1–1¼ hours
Oven: 180°C, 350°F, Gas Mark 4
A 1 kg (2 lb) loaf tin, or 2 × ½ kg (1 lb) tins, greased and base-lined

	METRIC	IMPERIAL
Soft margarine	170 g	6 oz
Caster sugar	170 g	6 oz
3 eggs		
Almond essence	¼ × 5 ml spoon	¼ teaspoon
A good pinch of salt		
Plain flour	255 g	9 oz
Baking powder	1 × 5 ml spoon	1 teaspoon
Glacé cherries	120–140 g	4–5 oz
Granulated sugar for sprinkling		

Cut the glacé cherries into quarters. If they are covered with sticky sugar syrup, wash them in warm water first and dry them. In a bowl, cream the margarine and sugar until very light and fluffy. Gradually beat in the eggs and almond essence. Now sift in the flour, salt, and baking powder, and fold in the quartered cherries, until everything is combined. Make sure you haven't left a thin layer of fat and sugar at the base of the bowl (a glass bowl helps here). Spoon the mixture carefully into the tin, slightly round the top of the cake with a knife and sprinkle with granulated sugar. If you wish, you could put four or five pieces of cherry on top as well. Place in the centre of a moderate oven and bake for 1 hour if using two small tins, or 1¼ hours for one large tin. The cake should be golden, well risen and yet fairly firm to the touch. Leave in tin for 2 minutes before turning out to cool on a wire tray.

To freeze: Wrap separately, or store in a lidded container.
To use: Thaw in wrapping for 3–4 hours at room temperature.

Mocha Marble Cake

This marble cake keeps amazingly well, and offers a super combination of chocolate, coffee and vanilla flavoured cake all in one. I think it is my own favourite marble cake. But I have also given instructions for a multi-coloured marble cake which children adore, and I often use it as the basis for a children's birthday cake.

Cooking time: 1 hour
Oven: 180°C, 350°F, Gas Mark 4
An 18 cm (7 in) round tin, greased and base-lined

	METRIC	IMPERIAL
Soft margarine	170 g	6 oz
Caster sugar	170 g	6 oz
Golden syrup	2 × 15 ml spoons	2 tablespoons
Vanilla essence	1 × 5 ml spoon	1 teaspoon
2 large eggs		
Plain flour	225 g	8 oz
Baking powder	1 × 5 ml spoon	1 teaspoon
A pinch of salt		
Milk	5 × 15 ml spoons	5 tablespoons
Instant coffee	2 × 5 ml spoons	2 teaspoons
Cocoa	2 × 15 ml spoons	2 tablespoons

Icing:

Icing sugar	225 g	8 oz
Butter or soft margarine	85 g	3 oz
Cocoa	2 × 15 ml spoons	2 tablespoons
Hot water	2 × 15 ml spoons	2 tablespoons
Instant coffee	1 × 5 ml spoon	1 teaspoon

Decoration:

Grated chocolate or 'Matchmakers' sticks	30 g	1 oz

Cream the margarine and sugar until light and fluffy. Add the syrup and vanilla and beat well again. Gradually add the beaten eggs to the mix and then the sieved flour, baking powder and salt alternately with four tablespoons (4 × 5 ml spoons) of the milk. Spoon about one-third of the mixture into the cake tin, leaving small islands all over the base of the tin. Spoon another third of the mixture into a small bowl and add the powdered coffee. Now spoon more islands into the tin, leaving a little mixture behind in the bowl. Into the last third of the mixture, sift the cocoa and mix in the remaining tablespoon (15 ml spoon) of milk. Spoon the chocolate mixture into the gaps in the cake tin and then finish off by spooning the coffee mixture into any remaining gaps. Don't worry if the surface of the cake isn't flat, as long as it's more or less the same thickness across the tin. Bake in the centre of a moderate oven for 1 hour until the cake sides are just shrinking away from the tin, and the top is firm. Leave to cool in the tin for 4 minutes before turning out on to a wire tray.

You can either coat the cake with melted chocolate, or make a coffee and chocolate flavoured icing. For the icing, mix the cocoa, coffee powder and hot water in a small cup. Sift the icing sugar into a bowl. Add the butter or soft margarine, and the mocha mixture from the cup. Beat well together for 1–2 minutes, until smooth and spreadable. Cover the sides and the top of the cake with icing, and either decorate with grated chocolate, or arrange coffee-flavoured 'Matchmakers' sticks in a suitable pattern.

To freeze: Store in a lidded plastic container so that the icing is not damaged.
To use: Thaw in container at room temperature for 4–5 hours.

Multi-Coloured Marble Cake

For this variation, follow the mocha marble cake recipe until you have a bowl of vanilla cake mixture. Now divide the mixture into as many parts as you have colours and flavourings. I usually use at least four, and mix them in small bowls or large mugs:

1 Vanilla: use the mixture as it is.
2 Raspberry: add 2–3 drops of cochineal or red colouring, and 2–3 drops of raspberry flavouring.
3 Peppermint: add 2–3 drops of green colouring, and 2–3 drops of peppermint essence.
4 Banana: add 2–3 drops of yellow colouring, and 2–3 drops of banana flavouring.
5 Orange: add 2–3 drops of orange colouring, and 2–3 drops of orange flavouring.
6 Chocolate: add 1 × 15 ml spoon (1 tablespoon) of cocoa and half this amount of milk.

Use a teaspoon to distribute the mixtures of your choice as islands all over the base of the tin, and then make a second layer so that the upper colour is different from the colour underneath. Bake in the centre of a moderate oven for 1 hour. Cool in the tin for 4 minutes before turning out on to a wire rack.

I usually decorate a multi-coloured marble cake with a creamy vanilla butter icing:

	METRIC	IMPERIAL
Icing sugar	225 g	8 oz
Butter or soft margarine	85 g	3 oz
Top of milk	1 × 15 ml spoon	1 tablespoon

2–3 drops of vanilla essence

Sift the icing sugar into a warmed bowl and beat in the margarine, vanilla essence and top of milk until the icing is pale, smooth and soft. Cover the sides and top of the cake with butter icing. All children seem to enjoy the cake even more if you round the decoration off with a small tube of Smarties (or dolly mixture). Gently press the Smarties, evenly-spaced, over the cake.

To freeze: Store the iced cake — without the Smarties — in a lidded container.
To use: Thaw in container at room temperature for 4–5 hours. Then decorate with Smarties or other sweets.

Honey Spice Cake with Apricot Topping

I see from my notebooks that I first devised this cake fifteen years ago, and it has become a firm favourite at home ever since.

Cooking time: 45 minutes
Oven: 190°C, 375°F, Gas Mark 5
An 18 or 20 cm (7 or 8 in) square tin, greased and base-lined

	METRIC	IMPERIAL
Soft margarine	225 g	8 oz
Light soft brown sugar	170 g	6 oz
Clear honey	55 g	2 oz
3 eggs		
Wholewheat plain flour	170 g	6 oz
Self-raising white flour	55 g	2 oz

Baking powder	$\frac{1}{2} \times 5$ ml spoon	$\frac{1}{2}$ teaspoon
Mixed spice	1×5 ml spoon	1 teaspoon
Topping:		
Dried apricots	115 g	4 oz
Water	150 ml	$\frac{1}{4}$ pint
Light soft brown sugar	1×15 ml spoon	1 tablespoon
Cornflour	2×5 ml spoons	2 teaspoons
Water	1×15 ml spoon	1 tablespoon

Cream the margarine and sugar until light and fluffy. Add the honey (warm it if it is set) and beat again. Gradually beat in the eggs and then sift in all the other ingredients, except the wholewheat flour. Fold in gently. Finally add the wholewheat flour and stir until combined. Spoon into the prepared tin and bake in the centre of a moderately hot oven for up to 45 minutes — until the cake is springy to the touch and just slightly shrinking from the sides. Turn out to cool on a wire rack.

While the cake is cooking, make the topping. Gently stew the dried apricots with the water for 25–30 minutes. Purée the apricots, either through a sieve or in an electric blender. In the saucepan mix the cornflour with the tablespoon (1×15 ml spoon) of water, add the sugar and the apricot purée. Cook gently, stirring all the time, and boil for 2 minutes. Remove from heat and allow to cool a little. Then spread it on to the honey spice cake while it is still warm on the wire rack.

To freeze: Store the cake, without topping, in a lidded container.
To use: Thaw in container at room temperature for 3–4 hours.

Almond Cake

I think that of all the flavours used in baking, almond is my own personal favourite. It also seems to be very popular with older people. Ground almonds are rather expensive, so I've worked out this recipe which uses only 55 g (2 oz) of them.

Cooking time: 1 hour
Oven: 180°C, 350°F, Gas Mark 4
A 1 kg (2 lb) loaf tin, or a 20 cm (8 in) round tin, greased and base-lined

	METRIC	IMPERIAL
Soft margarine	225 g	8 oz
Caster sugar	225 g	8 oz
4 eggs		
A few drops of almond essence		
Plain flour	225 g	8 oz
Baking powder	1 × 5 ml spoon	1 teaspoon
Ground almonds	55 g	2 oz
Flaked almonds	30 g	1 oz

Cream the margarine and sugar until really light and fluffy. Gradually beat in the eggs, add a little flour with the last egg and then the almond essence. Carefully fold in the sifted flour and baking powder, also the ground almonds and half of the flaked almonds. Spoon the mixture into the prepared tin. Sprinkle the rest of the flaked almonds on top. Bake in the centre of a moderate oven for 50–60 minutes. Leave in the tin for 2 minutes and then cool on a wire rack.

To freeze: This cake keeps well for a week without freezing. But to keep longer, store in a lidded container in the freezer.
To use: Thaw in the container at room temperature for 3–4 hours.

Coffee Walnut Cake

This is an all-time favourite with all ages. It's a marvellously quick all-in-one method which always gives good results. I always make it as a single-layer cake with coffee butter icing smoothed over the top and sides. To make it more of an occasion cake, you can split it in half and sandwich it with butter icing — or bake two cakes in slightly larger tins and sandwich those.

Cooking time: 45 minutes
Oven: nearly 190°C, 375°F, Gas Mark 5
A 20 cm (8 in) round tin, greased and base-lined

	METRIC	IMPERIAL
Soft margarine	140 g	5 oz
Caster sugar	140 g	5 oz
2 eggs		
Instant coffee powder	1 × 15 ml spoon	1 tablespoon
Salt	½ × 5 ml spoon	½ teaspoon
Baking powder	½ × 5 ml spoon	½ teaspoon
Chopped walnuts	45 g	1½ oz
Warm water	3 × 15 ml spoons	3 tablespoons
Self-raising flour	170 g	6 oz
Icing:		
Icing sugar	225 g	8 oz
Soft margarine or butter	85 g	3 oz
Instant coffee powder	2 × 5 ml spoons	2 teaspoons
Hot water	2 × 15 ml spoons	2 tablespoons
A few walnuts		

Simply put all the ingredients for the cake into a good-sized mixing bowl and beat well together with a wooden spoon or electric beater for up to 2 minutes. Everything will be well blended, smooth and of a soft dropping consistency. Pour or spoon the mixture into the prepared tin and bake above the centre of a moderate oven for 45 minutes, until the cake is just beginning to shrink away from the sides of the tin and the top is springy to the touch. Leave to cool in the tin for 2 minutes, and then cool on a wire rack.

For the icing, mix the powdered coffee and hot water in a small cup. Sieve the icing sugar into a warmed bowl, add the butter or margarine and liquid coffee and mix together well with a fork or electric beater until really smooth and soft. Spread the icing all over the cake (I usually start with the sides) and decorate the top either with walnut halves or chopped walnuts. You can either keep it for current eating in a plastic box, or freeze it.

To freeze: Store in a lidded plastic container.
To use: Thaw in container for 3–4 hours at room temperature.

Moist Chocolate Cake with Fudge Filling

I find this a useful recipe whenever I've run out of margarine. It uses corn oil instead, and this keeps the cake moist. Instead of a fudge filling, I sometimes sandwich the cake with whipped cream and pour melted chocolate over the top; or I sandwich the cake with a coffee or orange flavoured filling.

Cooking time: 35 minutes
Oven: 170°C, 325°F, Gas Mark 3
2 × 20 cm (8 in) sandwich tins, greased and base-lined

	METRIC	IMPERIAL
Plain flour	200 g	7 oz
Cocoa	4 × 15 ml spoons	4 tablespoons

Bicarbonate of soda	1 × 5 ml spoon	1 teaspoon
Baking powder	1 × 5 ml spoon	1 teaspoon
Light soft brown sugar	140 g	5 oz
Golden syrup	2 × 15 ml spoons	2 tablespoons
2 eggs		
Corn oil	150 ml	$\frac{1}{4}$ pint
Milk	150 ml	$\frac{1}{4}$ pint
Filling:		
Icing sugar	170 g	6 oz
Butter or soft margarine	45 g	$1\frac{1}{2}$ oz
Top of milk	1 × 15 ml spoon	1 tablespoon
Dark soft brown sugar	1 × 15 ml spoon	1 tablespoon

Sieve the flour, cocoa, bicarbonate of soda and baking powder into a good-sized mixing bowl. Add the sugar and mix together. Now, in a small bowl or jug, mix the eggs, syrup, oil and milk and beat well together with a fork. Pour this on to the flour mixture and beat all together to make a smooth batter. Pour it into the prepared tins and bake in the centre of a moderate oven for 35 minutes. Leave in the tin for 2 minutes before turning out to cool on a wire rack.

For the filling, sieve the icing sugar into a bowl and add the butter, milk and brown sugar. Put the bowl over 2 cm (1 in) of boiling water in a saucepan, and beat the filling until it is thoroughly blended. Remove from heat and allow to cool. Then sandwich the cakes with this fudge filling.

To freeze: Store in container in freezer.
To use: Thaw in container at room temperature for 3 hours.

Madeira Cake

This is an old-established favourite, and very popular on the cake stall with older folk. I really prefer to put long strips of candied peel on the top, but it's not always easy to buy. So I try to make sure I've always got some of my own — see the last chapter. This is my mother's recipe, and she says it came from her aunt. Her recipe uses butter, and I sometimes use it myself instead of soft margarine. It does give the cake a lovely flavour.

Cooking time: 1 hour
Oven: 180°C, 350°F, Gas Mark 4
An 18 cm (7 in) cake tin, greased and base-lined

	METRIC	IMPERIAL
Butter or soft margarine	140 g	5 oz
Caster sugar	140 g	5 oz
Finely grated lemon or orange rind	1 × 5 ml spoon	1 teaspoon
2 large eggs		
Plain flour	225 g	8 oz
A pinch of salt		
Baking powder	1 × 5 ml spoon	1 teaspoon
Milk	4 × 15 ml spoons	4 tablespoons
Strips of candied peel		

Cream the sugar and butter (or margarine) until really light and fluffy — it makes all the difference to the cake. Now gradually beat in the eggs and lemon (or orange) rind. Fold in the sieved flour, salt and baking powder with the milk. Spoon gently into the prepared cake tin and place the strips of candied peel on top. Bake in the centre of a moderate oven for 1 hour. Cool on a wire rack, after turning out.

To freeze: Wrap in plastic or store in container.
To use: Thaw at room temperature in container for 3 hours.

Light Ginger Cake

Not everyone likes the intense flavour of dark gingerbread. This recipe gives a cake with a milder flavour.

Cooking time: 45 minutes
Oven: 180°C, 350°F, Gas Mark 4
A 1 kg (2 lb) loaf tin, or two tins half this size, greased and base-lined

	METRIC	IMPERIAL
Soft margarine	170 g	6 oz
Light soft brown sugar	170 g	6 oz
3 eggs		
Plain flour	225 g	8 oz
Baking powder	1 × 5 ml spoon	1 teaspoon
Ground ginger	2 × 5 ml spoons	2 teaspoons
Ground cinnamon	$\frac{1}{2}$ × 5 ml spoon	$\frac{1}{2}$ teaspoon
Chopped candied peel	85 g	3 oz

Cream the margarine and sugar until light and fluffy. Gradually beat in the eggs. Sift the flour, baking powder and spices on to the egg mixture and fold in with the candied peel. Spoon into the prepared tin and bake in the centre of a moderate oven for 45–60 minutes, depending on the size of tin. Leave to cool in the tin for 2 minutes. Slip a knife down the sides of the tin, then turn cake out on a wire rack to cool.

To freeze: Wrap cakes separately and store in a container.
To use: Thaw in the container at room temperature for 3–4 hours.

Coconut Cake

I find this coconut cake keeps perfectly for a week in a tin, and is especially popular with older folk.

Cooking time: 1–1½ hours
Oven: 180°C, 350°F, Gas Mark 4
A 1 kg (2 lb) loaf tin, or two tins half this size, greased and base-lined

	METRIC	IMPERIAL
Soft margarine	170 g	6 oz
Caster sugar	170 g	6 oz
3 eggs		
Plain flour	200 g	7 oz
Baking powder	1 × 5 ml spoon	1 teaspoon
Desiccated coconut	85 g	3 oz
Granulated sugar for top		

Cream the margarine and sugar together until really pale, light and fluffy. Add the eggs, beating well after each addition. Sieve the flour and baking powder into a bowl, tip the coconut on top and stir. Now gradually fold the flour and coconut mixture into the cake mixture until well combined. Spoon the mixture into the tin, slightly round the top, and sprinkle with granulated sugar. Bake in the centre of a moderate oven for 1 hour with the smaller size tins, or for 1¼–1½ hours if using a single large tin, until the cake has a golden crust and is just beginning to shrink away from the sides of the tin. Leave in the tin for 3 minutes, then slip a knife between the cake and the tin on each side and turn out on a wire rack to cool.

To freeze: Wrap cakes separately and store in a container.
To use: Thaw in the wrapping and container at room temperature for 3 hours.

Streusel-Topped Cake

This is a marvellously quick cake to make by a rubbed-in method. It has a delicious topping and is even nicer served warm.

Cooking time: 45 minutes
Oven: 190°C, 375°F, Gas Mark 5
An 18 cm (7 in) square tin, or a 23 cm (9 in) spring-sided round tin, greased and base-lined

	METRIC	IMPERIAL
Plain flour	170 g	6 oz
Cornflour	55 g	2 oz
Baking powder	2 × 5 ml spoons	2 teaspoons
Salt	$\frac{1}{2}$ × 5 ml spoon	$\frac{1}{2}$ teaspoon
Caster sugar	115 g	4 oz
Soft margarine	115 g	4 oz
1 egg beaten with milk to make	150 ml	$\frac{1}{4}$ pint
Vanilla essence	$\frac{1}{2}$ × 5 ml spoon	$\frac{1}{2}$ teaspoon
Streusel topping:		
Plain flour	55 g	2 oz
Light soft brown sugar	55 g	2 oz
Cinnamon	2 × 5 ml spoon	2 teaspoons
Melted butter	55 g	2 oz

For the cake, sift the flour, cornflour, baking powder and salt into a bowl, stir in the sugar and then, using a knife, cut the soft margarine into the mixture until it is in very small pieces. (A fork helps here, too.) Pour in the egg and milk mixture and vanilla essence and mix well together with the fork. Pour into the prepared tin.

Now make the topping by mixing the flour, sugar and cinnamon together. Pour on the just-melted butter, and mix with a fork until crumbly. Sprinkle this over the top of the cake, and bake in the centre of a moderately hot oven for 45 minutes. Leave to cool in the tin for 5 minutes before turning out to cool on a rack.

To freeze: Wrap carefully, or store in a lidded plastic container.
To use: Thaw in the container at room temperature for 3 hours, and warm through in oven if desired.

Pineapple Walnut Cake

This is such a useful recipe when you find you have a single serving of pineapple chunks left over, and a few walnuts to hand. Complete with pineapple icing, it has a refreshing yet nutty taste.

Cooking time: 45–50 minutes
Oven: 180°C, 350°F, Gas Mark 4
An 18 cm (7 in) round tin, greased and base-lined

	METRIC	IMPERIAL
Soft margarine	115 g	4 oz
Caster sugar	115 g	4 oz
2 eggs		
Self-raising flour	140 g	5 oz
Chopped pineapple (2 rings)	85 g	3 oz
Chopped walnuts	45 g	1½ oz
Icing:		
Icing sugar	115 g	4 oz
Pineapple juice	1½ × 15 ml	1½ tablespoons
A knob of butter the size of a walnut		
1 drop of yellow colouring		
6 walnut halves or pieces, for decoration		

Cream the margarine and sugar together until fluffy and almost white. Gradually beat in the eggs. Fold in the sieved flour alternatively with the chopped pineapple and chopped walnuts. Turn into the prepared tin, level the top of the mixture with the back of a spoon and bake in the centre of a moderate oven for 45–50 minutes, until the cake is just starting to shrink away from the tin and the centre is springy to the touch. Cool in tin for 5 minutes before turning out on to a wire rack. Sieve the icing sugar into a bowl. In a small saucepan, gently warm the pineapple juice and butter. When the butter has melted, pour on to the icing sugar. Beat until smooth. Add just one drop of yellow colouring. Pour over cake and allow to drip down sides. Decorate the top with walnuts, halved or chopped.

To freeze: Store in a lidded container.
To use: Thaw in the container in cool temperature overnight, or for
  5–6 hours.

Chocolate Spice Cake with Vanilla Icing

This unusual chocolate cake comes from the West Indies. It contains dates, which give it a moistness that every good chocolate cake should have. Very few people seem to notice the dates — this always amuses me!

Cooking time: 30–45 minutes
Oven: 190°C, 375°F, Gas Mark 4
A 20 cm (8 in) cake tin, or two sandwich tins, greased and base-lined

	METRIC	IMPERIAL
Soft margarine	170 g	6 oz
Light soft brown sugar	140 g	5 oz
Golden syrup	2 × 15 ml spoons	2 tablespoons
3 eggs		
Plain flour	225 g	8 oz
Cocoa	2 × 15 ml spoons	2 tablespoons

Baking powder	3 × 5 ml spoons	3 teaspoons
Mixed spice	½ × 5 ml spoon	½ teaspoon
Nutmeg	½ × 5 ml spoon	½ teaspoon
Cinnamon	1 × 5 ml spoon	1 teaspoon
Chopped dates	115 g	4 oz
Vanilla:		
Icing sugar	285 g	10 oz
Butter or soft margarine	85 g	3 oz
Top of milk	1 × 15 ml spoon	
A few drops of vanilla essence		1 tablespoon
Half of a flaked chocolate bar for decoration		

Cream the margarine and sugar until light and fluffy. Add the syrup and beat well again. Gradually beat in the eggs. Sieve all the dry ingredients together in a bowl and then stir them carefully into the egg mixture. Add the chopped dates and stir again. Spoon the mixture into the tin, and bake in the centre of a moderately hot oven for 30 minutes if using two tins, or for 45 minutes with one, until the cake is springy to the touch. Cool on a wire tray. If you have used one tin, split the cake in half.

For the icing, sieve the icing sugar into a bowl. Add the butter (or margarine), the top of milk and a few drops of vanilla essence. With a fork or electric beater, mix it all together carefully, and then faster until the icing is soft and creamy. Sandwich the cake with icing and also coat the sides and the top. Decorate with crushed chocolate flake bar — half a bar will do.

To freeze: This cake freezes extremely well. Store in a container to prevent damage to the icing.
To use: Thaw in the container at room temperature for 3–4 hours.

Caraway Seed Cake

Seed cake has been baked and eaten in this country for over 300 years. In Victorian times it was served mid-morning, perhaps with a glass of madeira. Caraway seed cake is rarely made today, but it's still very much appreciated, particularly by older people.

Cooking time: 45–55 minutes
Oven: 180°C, 350°F, Gas Mark 4
A 1 kg (2 lb) loaf tin, or two tins half this size, greased and base-lined

	METRIC	IMPERIAL
Soft margarine	150 g	6 oz
Caster sugar	150 g	6 oz
3 eggs		
Plain flour, sifted	200 g	8 oz
Baking powder	1 × 5 ml spoon	1 teaspoon
A good pinch of salt		
Ground almonds	1 × 15 ml spoon	1 tablespoon
Caraway seeds	3 × 5 ml spoons	3 teaspoons
Milk	1 × 15 ml spoon	1 tablespoon

Cream the margarine and sugar until light and fluffy. Gradually beat in the eggs and the caraway seeds. Fold in the sifted flour, baking powder, salt and ground almonds with the milk. Spoon into the prepared tin and bake in the centre of a moderate oven for 45–55 minutes depending upon size of tin. Leave to rest in tin for 2 minutes, then loosen sides with a knife and turn out on to a wire rack to cool.

To freeze: Wrap cakes separately and store in closed containers.
To use: Thaw in containers at room temperature for 3–4 hours.

Chocolate and Ginger Cake

I created this cake one January, when I still had some stem ginger in syrup left from Christmas. I've always thought of it as a winter cake, but it has a light texture and an exciting taste.

Cooking time: 40–55 minutes
Oven: 180°C, 350°F, Gas Mark 4
A 20 cm (8 in) round tin or two 17 cm (6½ in) round tins to make two cakes. They must be greased and base-lined

	METRIC	IMPERIAL
Dark soft brown sugar	170 g	6 oz
Soft margarine	170 g	6 oz
3 large eggs		
Cocoa	4 × 15 ml spoons	4 tablespoons
Hot water	4 × 15 ml spoons	4 tablespoons
Self-raising flour	170 g	6 oz
Baking powder	½ × 5 ml spoon	½ teaspoon
Chopped preserved stem ginger	55 g	2 oz
Icing:		
Icing sugar	170 g	6 oz
Ginger syrup	2 × 15 ml spoons	2 tablespoons
Some pieces of preserved ginger		

Cream the sugar and margarine together until fluffy. Gradually beat in the eggs. Now in a small bowl or cup, mix the cocoa to a paste with the hot water and add to the egg mixture. Beat in well. Sift the flour and baking powder into the mixture and fold in with the chopped ginger. Spoon into the tin and bake just above the centre of a moderate oven (40 minutes for smaller cakes, 55 minutes for larger), until the cake is springy to the touch and just starting to shrink away from the sides of the tin. Leave in the tin for 2 minutes, before cooling on a wire rack.

75

For the icing, start by sieving the icing sugar into a bowl. Then add the syrup from the jar of preserved ginger, and mix to a pouring icing. (You may need to add a teaspoon — 1 × 5 ml spoon — of hot water too.) Pour over the top of the cake and allow to drip down the sides. Decorate the top with pieces of preserved or candied ginger.

To freeze: Store in a closed plastic container.
To use: Thaw in the container at room temperature for 3–4 hours.

Iced Honey Cake

This recipe was given to me by a Devon bee-keeper, and I find it really good. It's mixed straight in the saucepan, and is therefore very quick. Honey keeps a cake moist, so this one stays fresh quite a time, which makes it very useful, I find, for the school holidays.

Cooking time: 45 minutes
Oven: 180°C, 350°F, Gas Mark 4
A 20 cm (8 in) square tin, greased and base-lined

	METRIC	IMPERIAL
Light soft brown sugar	115 g	4 oz
Soft margarine	140 g	5 oz
Honey	170 g	6 oz
Water	1 × 15 ml spoon	1 tablespoon
2 eggs		
Self-raising flour	200 g	7 oz
Icing:		
Icing sugar	115 g	4 oz
Clear honey	1 × 15 ml spoon	1 tablespoon
Water	1 × 15 ml spoon	1 tablespoon

Gently heat the sugar, margarine, honey and water in a good-sized saucepan. Remove from the heat as soon as the margarine has melted. Beat in the eggs and stir in the sifted flour thoroughly. Spoon this mixture into the prepared tin and bake in the centre of a moderate oven for 45 minutes, until firm to the touch and just shrinking from the sides of the tin. Turn out and cool on a wire rack.

Ice while still just warm. Mix the sieved icing sugar with the honey and water, and pour over the cake in trickles.

To freeze: I usually freeze the cake un-iced in a closed container.
To use: Thaw in the container at room temperature for 3 hours, then ice or sprinkle with demerara sugar before serving.

Featherlight Chocolate Cake

This is an American recipe which combines chocolate with cinnamon and coffee to give a very well-rounded flavour. I really like to cook this cake in a ring mould or a brioche tin, and I sometimes use it as a basis for tipsy cake.

Cooking time: 1¼ hours
Oven: 170°C, 325°F, Gas Mark 3
A 20 cm (8 in) ring tin, or a fluted brioche tin, greased

	METRIC	IMPERIAL
Plain chocolate	55 g	2 oz
Self-raising flour	155 g	5½ oz
Baking powder	1 × 5 ml spoon	1 teaspoon
Cinnamon	¼ × 5 ml spoon	¼ teaspoon
Salt	¼ × 5 ml spoon	¼ teaspoon
Instant coffee powder	1 × 5 ml spoon	1 teaspoon
Caster sugar	155 g	5½ oz
3 egg yolks		

Corn oil	3 × 15 ml spoons	3 tablespoons
Water	3 × 15 ml spoons	3 tablespoons
Vanilla essence	1 × 5 ml spoon	1 teaspoon
3 egg whites		
Icing:		
Icing sugar	115 g	4 oz
Instant coffee powder	1 × 5 ml spoon	1 teaspoon
Cocoa	2 × 5 ml spoons	2 teaspoons
Soft margarine	55 g	2 oz
Hot water	1 × 15 ml spoon	1 tablespoon

Melt the chocolate in a small bowl over hot water. Sieve the flour, baking powder, cinnamon, salt and coffee powder into a bowl. Stir in the sugar. Add the egg yolks, oil and water, vanilla essence, and beat well with a wooden spoon for 1–2 minutes. Now beat in the melted chocolate until well combined. In another bowl, whisk the egg whites until stiff, then pour the chocolate mixture into the whites, folding in with a metal spoon. Gently spoon into the prepared tin and bake in the centre of a slow oven for up to $1\frac{1}{4}$ hours, until the cake feels springy to the touch. Turn out to cool on a wire rack.

For the icing, sift the sugar, coffee and cocoa into a bowl, add the margarine and mix well with a fork. Gradually add the hot water and beat until soft and spreadable. Coat the top and sides of the cake, leaving a pattern of peaks.

To freeze: Store in a lidded container. (I once kept one for a whole year, and it was excellent!)
To use: Thaw in the container overnight at room temperature.

Fresh Orange Ring

This is a perfect cake or pudding for a sweltering June day. For a dinner party, fill the ring with strawberries tossed in caster sugar and orange juice.

Cooking time: 45 minutes
Oven: 180°C, 350°F, Gas Mark 4
A ring cake tin of about 20 cm (8 in) diameter, well greased

	METRIC	IMPERIAL
Soft margarine	170 g	6 oz
Caster sugar	170 g	6 oz
3 eggs		
The grated rind of one orange		
Self-raising flour	170 g	6 oz
Orange syrup:		
Caster sugar	115 g	4 oz
The juice of 2 oranges, or a small glass of frozen or bottled orange juice		

Cream the margarine and caster sugar until really light, fluffy and creamy. How high the cake rises really depends upon this operation, so do the best you can — it's very easy, of course, with an electric beater. Gradually beat in the eggs and finely grated orange rind. Lastly, gently fold in the sifted flour. Spoon into the ring cake tin and level the top of the mixture. Bake just above the centre of a moderate oven for 45 minutes. Leave in the tin for 2 minutes, and then turn out to cool on a wire rack.

Now wash the ring tin out well and dry it. When the cake is cool put it back in the tin. Make the syrup by dissolving the sugar in 2 × 15 ml spoons (2 tablespoons) of hot water over very gentle heat. Remove from heat and add the orange juice. Stir well, and then start to pour it in a trickle over the orange cake. You can also make a few holes with a cocktail stick if you wish. Gradually the cake will absorb all the syrup. Leave until cold, then carefully tip the cake out of the tin and on to a plate. It can be served plain like this, but I prefer to pipe rosettes of whipped cream over the cake and set it aside for 2 hours to allow the flavour to mellow.

To freeze: I have frozen the finished cream-decorated cake overnight, but it is better to freeze the unsoaked ring cake in a lidded container.
To use: Thaw in container at room temperature for 3 hours, then soak with syrup as above.

Lightning Walnut Cake with Vanilla Filling

This is such a very quick all-in-one cake to make, that I find I'm always recommending it to friends — of all ages, from five upwards!

Cooking time: 35–45 minutes
Oven: 180°C, 350°F, Gas Mark 4
A 20 cm (8 in) round tin about 8 cm (3 in) deep, or two 18 cm (7 in) sandwich tins, greased and base-lined

	METRIC	IMPERIAL
Self-raising flour	170 g	6 oz
Baking powder	1 × 5 ml spoon	1 teaspoon
Caster sugar	170 g	6 oz
Soft margarine	170 g	6 oz
3 large eggs		
Finely-chopped walnuts	55 g	2 oz
Vanilla butter cream filling:		
Icing sugar	115 g	4 oz
Butter or soft margarine	55 g	2 oz
Top of milk	1–2 × 5 ml spoons	1–2 teaspoons

A few drops of vanilla essence

For the cake, put all the ingredients into a bowl, and with a fork or electric beater, mix all together really thoroughly for 1 minute. Spoon the mixture into one or two tins, and bake in the centre of a moderate oven for 35 minutes for sandwich tins, and 45 minutes for the larger cake. Turn out and cool on a wire tray.

For the icing, mix the sifted icing sugar with the butter, milk and vanilla until soft and spreadable. Sandwich the cake with the filling, and dust the top of the cake with caster sugar. This cake has the extra advantage of freezing very well.

To freeze: Wrap or store in a lidded container.
To use: Thaw in the container at room temperature for 3 hours.

Marmalade Cake

This is a very popular winter cake for serving after buttered crumpets at a fireside tea. I use my home-made Seville marmalade, and it seems to help the cake to keep.

Cooking time: 1 hour
Oven: 180°C, 350°F, Gas Mark 4
A 20 cm (8 in) or 23 cm (9 in) round tin, greased and base-lined

	METRIC	IMPERIAL
Soft margarine	170 g	6 oz
Golden syrup	170 g	6 oz
2 eggs		
Orange marmalade	5 × 15 ml spoons	5 tablespoons
Self-raising flour	340 g	12 oz
Baking powder	1 × 5 ml spoon	1 teaspoon
Nutmeg	1 × 5 ml spoon	1 teaspoon
Cinnamon	1 × 5 ml spoon	1 teaspoon
Ground cloves	$\frac{1}{4}$ × 5 ml spoon	$\frac{1}{4}$ teaspoon
Milk	150 ml	$\frac{1}{4}$ pint
Demerara sugar	30 g	1 oz
Cornflakes	30 g	1 oz

Beat the margarine and syrup together, and gradually add the eggs, beating well. Mix in the marmalade, flour, baking powder and spices with enough milk to give a stiff consistency. Spoon into the prepared tin and level the top of the mixture. Sprinkle the top with the crushed cornflakes and demerara sugar. Bake in the centre of a moderate oven for 1 hour, until the cake is just shrinking away from the tin. Leave in the tin for 5 minutes before turning out to cool on a wire rack.

To freeze: Wrap or store in a container.
To use: Thaw in the container at room temperature for 3–4 hours.

GERALDENE HOLT'S CAKE STALL

FRUIT CAKES

The world is divided into those who, when asked to think of a cake, think of a creamy, rich chocolate gâteau, and those who conjure up a succulent, aromatic fruit cake. Fruit cakes don't stay uneaten at any time of the year, but they can help a lot when one has to keep going through a cold winter. When November is here and we feel the need for inner solace, I always remember that Truman Capote short story that starts with the observation, 'It's fruitcake weather, buddy!'

I have included not only our family fruit cake recipes, but also all my own favourite recipes which make use of fruit, like pineapple-upside-down cake. I hope you enjoy eating them.

Harvest Cake

This is my mother's most-baked fruit cake — always reliable and welcomed. I find it a tremendous seller on the cake stall, and I think it is the easiest cake of all to make.

Cooking time: 1¾ hours
Oven: 170°C, 325°F, Gas Mark 3
A 20 cm (8 in) round or square cake tin, greased and base-lined

	METRIC	IMPERIAL
Soft margarine	225 g	8 oz
Caster sugar	225 g	8 oz
4 eggs, beaten		
Plain flour	340 g	12 oz
Baking powder	1 × 5 ml spoon	1 teaspoon
Mixed raisins, sultanas, currants	450 g	1 lb
Glacé cherries, quartered	115 g	4 oz

The method, incredibly enough, is simply to put all the ingredients into a large bowl (slightly warmed in cold weather) and mix them all together well until a stiff dough results. Spoon the mixture into the prepared tin and bake just below the centre of a moderate oven for 1 hour 50 minutes. Leave to cool in the tin for 15 minutes, then turn out on to a wire rack and peel off the paper. This cake keeps marvellously in a tin for up to a month.

To freeze: Simply wrap in plastic or store in a lidded container.
To use: Thaw in the wrapping at room temperature for 6–8 hours, or overnight.

Light Fruit Cake

This is the cake I always like to have as a standby in the cake tin or freezer. It is not too rich, and always has the same fresh taste.

Cooking time: 1–1½ hours
Oven: 180°C, 350°F, Gas Mark 4
A 1 kg (2 lb) loaf tin, or two ½ kg (1 lb) loaf tins, greased and base-lined

	METRIC	IMPERIAL
Soft margarine	170 g	6 oz
Caster sugar	170 g	6 oz
3 eggs		
Vanilla essence	¼ × 5 ml spoon	¼ teaspoon
Plain flour	255 g	9 oz
Baking powder	1 × 5 ml spoon	1 teaspoon
A pinch of salt		
Mixed dried fruit	340 g	12 oz
Granulated sugar for top	2 × 5 ml spoon	2 teaspoons

Cream the margarine and sugar until really light and fluffy. Beat in the eggs gradually, adding a little flour with the last egg. Add the vanilla essence and mix in the sifted flour and baking powder with the salt and the fruit. Spoon into the tin, and slightly round the top of the cake. Sprinkle with granulated sugar and bake in the centre of a moderate oven for 1 hour (smaller tin) or 1½ hours (larger tin). Leave to cool in the tin for 5 minutes before turning out to cool on a wire rack.

To freeze: Wrap or pack the cakes separately.
To use: Thaw in container at room temperature for 5 hours.

Date Cake

I first devised this cake for my brother, who is crazy about dates.
Now everyone likes it.

Cooking time: 50 minutes
Oven: 180°C, 350°F, Gas Mark 4
A 1 kg (2 lb) loaf tin, or two half this size, greased and base-lined

	METRIC	IMPERIAL
Chopped dates	170 g	6 oz
Boiling water	75 ml	⅛ pint
Dark soft brown sugar	170 g	6 oz
Soft margarine	170 g	6 oz
3 eggs		
Plain flour	255 g	9 oz
Baking powder	1 × 5 ml spoon	1 teaspoon
Nutmeg	½ × 5 ml spoon	½ teaspoon
Chopped dates	85 g	3 oz
4 crushed allspice berries		
Icing:		
Icing sugar	115 g	4 oz
Hot water	2 × 15 ml spoons	2 tablespoons

In a small bowl, pour the boiling water on to the 170 g (6 oz) of
chopped dates and leave to soften. In a larger bowl, cream the
margarine and sugar until light and fluffy. Now beat in the 170 g
(6 oz) of softened dates, and then the eggs, until well combined.
Sift in the flour, baking powder and nutmeg, and mix together.
Lastly mix in the 85 g (3 oz) of chopped dates and the crushed
allspice. Spoon into the prepared tin and bake in the centre of a
moderate oven for 50 minutes. Turn on to a wire rack to cool.

Make the icing by sifting the icing sugar and mixing it with
enough hot water to make a pouring icing. Use the spoon to trail
lines of icing backwards and forwards across the cake in a
random pattern.

To freeze: Wrap or store in container.
To use: Thaw in container at room temperature for 3 hours.

Anna's Banana Cake with Lemon Icing

This delicious banana cake comes from a friend with five children, and they can demolish it in a flash. But it does keep beautifully moist for several days.

Cooking time: 45 minutes
Oven: 180°C, 350°F, Gas Mark 4
A 17 cm (6½ in) round tin, greased and base-lined

	METRIC	IMPERIAL
Soft margarine	85 g	3 oz
Caster sugar	85 g	3 oz
1 large mashed banana		
A squeeze of lemon juice		
1 large egg		
Self-raising flour	115 g	4 oz
Icing:		
Icing sugar	85 g	3 oz
Lemon juice	1 × 15 ml spoon	1 teaspoon

1–2 drops of yellow colouring

Cream the margarine and sugar until light and fluffy. Add the mashed banana and lemon juice and beat well. Mix in the egg, then fold in the sifted flour. Spoon into the prepared tin and bake in the centre of a moderate oven for 45 minutes. Turn out to cool on a wire rack.

Mix the sifted icing sugar and lemon juice to make a pouring icing, and add 1–2 drops of yellow colouring to give a pale yellow colour. Pour over the cake and allow to set. Decorate with grated lemon rind or small pieces of candied lemon slice. This cake is just as delicious with orange icing.

To freeze: Store in a lidded container.
To use: Thaw in the container at room temperature for 3 hours.

Raisin Cake

This is a good family fruit cake, and the muscatel flavour of the raisins can be further brought out by soaking them in a little sherry.

Cooking time: 1–1½ hours
Oven: 180°C, 350°F, Gas Mark 4
A 1 kg (2 lb) loaf tin, or two tins half this size, greased and base-lined

	METRIC	IMPERIAL
Soft margarine	170 g	6 oz
Light soft brown sugar	170 g	6 oz
3 eggs		
Plain flour	285 g	10 oz
Baking powder	1 × 5 ml spoon	1 teaspoon
A pinch of salt		
Sherry or milk	2 × 15 ml spoons	2 tablespoons
Seedless raisins	340 g	12 oz

Cream the margarine and the soft brown sugar until light and fluffy. Beat in the eggs then sift in the flour, baking powder and salt. Fold in the flour alternately with the raisins (which you can, if you wish, soak beforehand in sherry) and with the sherry or milk. Spoon into the prepared tin and bake in the centre of a moderate oven for 1 hour (smaller tin) or 1½ hours (larger tin) — until the cake is well risen, golden and just starting to shrink from the tin. Leave in the tin for 5 minutes before cooling on a wire rack.

To freeze: Wrap or store in a container.
To use: Thaw in the container at room temperature for 3 hours.

Pineapple-Upside-Down Cake

As a child this was my favourite cake, not least because I was given the job of placing the pineapple and cherries in the cake tin. It's also a good cake to use as a pudding — especially served hot, with pouring cream.

Cooking time: 40–50 minutes
Oven: 180°C, 350°F, Gas Mark 4
A 20–23 cm (8–9 in) square tin, greased and base-lined

	METRIC	IMPERIAL
Butter	1 × 15 ml spoon	1 tablespoon
Light soft brown sugar	2 × 15 ml spoons	2 tablespoons
9 pineapple slices		
18 maraschino cherries		
(or large glacé cherries)		
Soft margarine	170 g	6 oz
Caster sugar	170 g	6 oz
3 eggs		
Self-raising flour	200 g	7 oz
A little pineapple juice		

First take a small saucepan, and gently melt the butter in it. Mix in the sugar and then pour into the base of the cake tin. Arrange the pineapple rings in the base, and place the cherries in the centre of each ring and between the rings. (If you cut the cherries, make sure you put the cut side uppermost.)

Cream the margarine and sugar until light and fluffy. Then beat in the eggs well. Sift in the flour and fold into the mixture with a little pineapple juice or milk, until the mixture is of soft dropping consistency. Spoon the mixture carefully on to the pineapple layer. Level the top, and bake in the centre of a moderate oven for 40–50 minutes, until the cake is springy to the touch. Leave in the tin for 5 minutes, and then turn on to a wire rack to cool, or straight on to a large flat platter if you are serving it at once.

To freeze: Store in a lidded container.
To use: Thaw in the container at room temperature for 3 hours; then heat through in a hot oven for 15 minutes.

Cider Fruit Cake from Devon

I was given this recipe by a Devon farmer's wife. I use the local cider for soaking the fruit overnight, but any sweet cider is fine and it will give the cake an unusual but delightful flavour.

Cooking time: 70 minutes
Oven: 180°C, 350°F, Gas Mark 4
A 20 cm (8 in) round tin, or two 17 cm (6½ in) round tins, greased and base-lined

	METRIC	IMPERIAL
Raisins	85 g	3 oz
Sultanas	85 g	3 oz
Currants	85 g	3 oz
Sweet cider	4 × 15 ml spoons	4 tablespoons
Soft margarine	170 g	6 oz
Light soft brown sugar	170 g	6 oz
3 eggs		
Self-raising flour	225 g	8 oz
Mixed spice	1 × 5 ml spoon	1 teaspoon

First soak the dried fruit overnight in a bowl with the cider. The fruit will absorb the cider.

Cream the margarine and sugar until light and fluffy. Gradually add the eggs, beating each in well with a little flour. Sift in the rest of the flour and mixed spice, folding this into the mixture alternately with the cider-soaked fruit. Spoon into the prepared tin, and bake in the centre of a moderate oven for 55 minutes (smaller tin) or 70 minutes (larger tin). Leave in the tin for 4 minutes before turning out to cool on a wire rack. This cake keeps well in a tin for a week.

To freeze: Store in a lidded container or wrap in film.
To use: Thaw in the container at room temperature for 3 hours.

Maraschino Cherry Cake with 7-Minute Frosting

I devised this cake to welcome my daughter's French exchange partner. It also makes a good birthday cake for a girl, since this is a pink cake with thick fluffy frosting. I usually make the cake the day before, and then sandwich it and cover it with frosting about 3 hours before serving.

Cooking time: 40 minutes
Oven: 180°C, 350°F, Gas Mark 4
2 × 18 cm (7 in) sandwich tins, greased and base-lined

	METRIC	IMPERIAL
Caster sugar	170 g	6 oz
Soft margarine or butter	170 g	6 oz
2 eggs		
2 egg yolks		
Maraschino syrup	2 × 15 ml spoons	2 tablespoons
A few drops of cochineal red colouring		
Self-raising flour	170 g	6 oz
Ground almonds	30 g	1 oz
Maraschino cherries, quartered (or glacé cherries)	85 g	3 oz
Frosting:		
Granulated sugar	340 g	12 oz
2 egg whites		
Cream of tartar	¼ × 5 ml spoon	¼ teaspoon
Water	4 × 15 ml spoons	4 tablespoons
Vanilla essence	1 × 5 ml spoon	1 teaspoon
Six cherries for decoration, cut into eighths		

Cream the sugar and margarine until really fluffy. Gradually beat in the yolks and eggs, and then the syrup. If the mixture doesn't look pink enough, add a few drops of cochineal. Then fold in the sieved flour, ground almonds and quartered cherries. Divide between the two prepared tins and bake in the centre of a moderate oven for 40 minutes, then turn out on to a wire rack.

For the frosting, put a large heatproof bowl over 2 cm (1 in) of simmering water in a saucepan. Put all the sugar, water, egg whites and cream of tartar into the bowl. Whisk with a hand-held beater for 7 minutes — use the clock or timer. Remove from the heat and beat for another 4–5 minutes, until the frosting is thick and stands in peaks. Sandwich the cakes generously with the frosting and then cover the top and sides of the cake. Decorate with cherries, and leave to set for 3 hours.

To freeze: Store cake only in a lidded container.
To use: Thaw in container at room temperature for 2 hours then frost the cake.

Pineapple Fruit Cake

This is a lovely Australian cake which uses crushed pineapple. It gives the cake a sparkling fresh flavour, and makes it wonderfully moist.

Cooking time: 2 hours
Oven: 170°C, 325°F, Gas Mark 3
A 20 cm (8 in) round cake tin, greased and base-lined

	METRIC	IMPERIAL
Soft margarine	140 g	5 oz
Light soft brown sugar	140 g	5 oz
2 large eggs		
Self-raising flour	225 g	8 oz
Baking powder	½ × 5 ml spoon	½ teaspoon
Mixed dried fruit	400 g	14 oz
Glacé cherries, quartered	85 g	3 oz
Chopped candied peel	85 g	3 oz
Drained crushed pineapple	225 g	8 oz

Cream the margarine and sugar until light and fluffy. Beat the eggs in well. Sift the flour and baking powder into the mixture, and fold in with the fruit, cherries, peel and pineapple. Make sure everything is well combined. Spoon into the prepared tin and bake in the centre of a very moderate oven for 2 hours, until the cake is golden colour and shrinking slightly away from the tin. Leave in the tin for 15 minutes before turning out to cool on a wire tray.

This cake will keep well for 1–2 weeks in a plastic container, especially if kept in a fridge.

To freeze: Wrap in film or store in a lidded container.
To use: Thaw in the container at room temperature for 5–6 hours.

Clyst William Cake

I devised this cake two days after we moved to our Devon farmhouse, and it's now a very popular cake with everyone. Clyst means spring, and we have a spring-fed well in the corner of the kitchen.

Cooking time: 1 hour
Oven: 170°C, 325°F, Gas Mark 3
A 1 kg (2 lb) loaf tin, or two tins half this size, greased and base-lined

	METRIC	IMPERIAL
Plain flour	285 g	10 oz
Demerara sugar	170 g	6 oz
Soft margarine	170 g	6 oz
Mixed dried fruit	400 g	14 oz
Glacé cherries	55 g	2 oz
Mixed spice	1 × 5 ml spoon	1 teaspoon
Baking powder	1 × 5 ml spoon	1 teaspoon
3 eggs		
Black treacle	1 × 15 ml spoon	1 tablespoon

Put the flour and sugar in a bowl and cut the margarine into the mixture with a knife. Use your fingertips to rub the margarine into the mixture until it looks like breadcrumbs. Now add the dried fruit, quartered cherries, spice and baking powder. Beat the eggs with the treacle and mix this in too. Combine all together well and spoon into the prepared tin. Bake below the centre of a very moderate oven for 1 hour (smaller tins) or 1½ hours (larger tin). Leave in the tin for 5 minutes before turning out to cool on a wire rack.

To freeze: Wrap separately, or store in container.
To use: Thaw in container at room temperature for 5–6 hours.

Tropical Fruit Cake

I like the unusual flavour which dried apricots, prunes and dried fruit salad give to this cake.

Cooking time: 50 minutes
Oven: 180°C, 350°F, Gas Mark 4
An 18 cm (7 in) round cake tin, greased and base-lined

	METRIC	IMPERIAL
Soft margarine	115 g	4 oz
Caster sugar	115 g	4 oz
2 eggs		
Self-raising flour	170 g	6 oz
Dried fruit salad	140 g	5 oz
Red glacé cherries	55 g	2 oz
Angelica	30 g	1 oz
Mixed candied peel	30 g	1 oz
Honey for the glaze	1 × 5 ml spoon	1 teaspoon

First chop the dried fruit in the fruit salad — apricots, prunes, pears, apples — with the glacé cherries, angelica and mixed peel. Now cream the margarine and caster sugar until light and fluffy. Then beat in the eggs well. Fold in the sifted flour with the chopped fruit. Spoon into the prepared tin and bake in the centre of a moderate oven for 50 minutes, until the cake is golden and springy to the touch. Leave it in the tin for 5 minutes before turning out to cool on a wire rack. Brush the top of the cake with honey while it is still warm.

To freeze: Wrap, or store in a lidded container.
To use: Thaw in the container at room temperature for 4 hours.

Sultana and Almond Cake

The secret of this delicious cake is to soak the sultanas in the almond syrup until they are fat and plumped up. Ever since I created this cake it has proved to be tremendously popular, both at home and at the stall.

Cooking time: 50–75 minutes
Oven: 180°C, 350°F, Gas Mark 4
2 × 1 kg (2 lb) loaf tins, or four ½ kg (1 lb) loaf tins, greased and base-lined

	METRIC	IMPERIAL
Granulated sugar	30 g	1 oz
Boiling water	150 ml	¼ pint
Almond essence	¼ × 5 ml spoon	¼ teaspoon
Sultanas	450 g	16 oz
Caster sugar	55 g	2 oz
Light soft brown sugar	140 g	5 oz
Soft margarine	225 g	8 oz
3 large eggs		
Plain flour	340 g	12 oz
Baking powder	1 × 5 ml spoon	1 teaspoon
Flaked almonds	15 g	½ oz

First take a bowl and in it dissolve the sugar in the boiling water. Allow to cool a little. Stir in the almond essence and then the sultanas. Stir well and allow to steep for 1–2 hours or overnight.

Cream the soft margarine and the sugars. Beat in the eggs, sift in the flour and baking powder and then stir in the soaked sultanas. Mix all together well. Spoon into the prepared tins and sprinkle the tops of the cakes with the flaked almonds. Bake in the centre of a moderate oven for 50 minutes (smaller tins) or 75 minutes (larger tins). Leave in the tin for 5 minutes before turning out to cool on a wire rack.

To freeze: Wrap separately, or store in a lidded container.
To use: Thaw in the container at room temperature for 4–5 hours.

German Orange Cake

This orange cake comes from Nuremberg — a very important centre for German baking. It uses the unusual combination of orange and rum.

Cooking time: 45 minutes
Oven: 170°C, 325°F, Gas Mark 3
A 20 cm (8 in) tin — ideally one with a spring form — greased and base-lined

	METRIC	IMPERIAL
3 egg yolks		
Caster sugar	85 g	3 oz
Rum	1 × 15 ml spoon	1 tablespoon
The grated rind and juice of one orange		
Flour	85g	3 oz
Melted butter	55 g	2 oz
3 egg whites		

Cube sugar	55 g	2 oz
Icing:		
1 strip of orange peel		
Water	2 × 15 ml spoons	2 tablespoons
Rum	1 × 15 ml spoon	1 tablespoon
Icing sugar	225 g	8 oz
8 walnut halves		

First of all, pare a strip of peel from the orange and put it in a small bowl or mug with the cube sugar and the tablespoon of water. Every so often give it a stir, so that the cubes absorb the zest from the peel for the icing.

To make the cake, put the egg yolks and caster sugar in a bowl and beat or whisk (use an electric beater if you have one) the mixture until it is pale and frothy. Add the finely grated orange rind, orange juice and the rum. Stir together, and add alternately the sifted flour and the butter. In another bowl whisk the egg whites until stiff and standing in peaks. Then, with a metal spoon, gently fold the egg whites into the egg mixture. When all is combined, spoon into the prepared tin and bake in the centre of a very moderate oven until well risen and springy to the touch. Leave in tin for 3 minutes before turning out on a wire rack.

For the icing, take a saucepan and in it very gently heat the cube sugar, orange peel and water from the mug. Stir until the sugar is dissolved. Remove from heat, extract the orange peel and discard. Add the rum and the sieved icing sugar, and mix to a pouring icing. Pour over the top of the cake and allow to dribble down the sides. If serving straight away, decorate with walnuts, or segments of fresh orange, or candied orange slices.

To freeze: Store in a lidded container, plain or iced.
To use: Thaw in container at room temperature for 4 hours. Then decorate.

Dundee Cake

This is one of the best traditional British cakes. I like to see a Dundee cake covered in split almonds arranged in radiating circles. The cake is always improved by keeping it for at least a week, to allow the flavours to mellow. This is a super cake to give as a present.

Cooking time: about 2 hours
Oven: 170°C, 325°F, Gas Mark 3
An 18 cm (7 in) round cake tin, greased and base-lined

	METRIC	IMPERIAL
Soft margarine or butter	170 g	6 oz
Light soft brown sugar, or caster sugar	170 g	6 oz
3 eggs		
The finely-grated rind of one orange (or lemon)		
Plain flour	255 g	9 oz
Baking powder	1 × 5 ml spoon	1 teaspoon
A good pinch of salt		
Mixed spice (optional)	1 × 5 ml spoon	1 teaspoon
Sultanas	170 g	6 oz
Raisins (seedless)	115 g	4 oz
Currants	115 g	4 oz
Glacé cherries (quartered)	85 g	3 oz
Chopped candied peel	55 g	2 oz
Ground almonds	30 g	1 oz
A little milk		
Blanched split almonds	30–55 g	1–2 oz

Cream the margarine and sugar until light and fluffy. Gradually beat in the eggs and grated orange rind. Sift the flour, baking powder, salt and spice into the bowl and fold in gently with the mixed fruit, peel and ground almonds. The mixture for a Dundee cake should be fairly stiff, but add a little milk if the mix is difficult to stir. Spoon into the prepared tin and level the top of the cake with the back of a spoon. Then, starting at the outside edge of the cake, arrange the split almonds in a ring, not too close together. Arrange another ring inside that one, and then a third and final ring. Just place three or four split almonds in the very centre. Bake in the middle of a very moderate oven for 2 hours. Test with a wooden kebab stick or skewer; when it comes out clean, remove cake from oven. Leave in tin for 20 minutes, then turn out on a wire rack. Store in a lidded tin or plastic box.

To freeze: If you are keeping the cake for a short time only, there is no need to freeze a Dundee cake. Otherwise, wrap it carefully before freezing, or store in a lidded container.
To use: Thaw in wrapping at room temperature for 6–8 hours, or overnight.

Apricot and Almond Cake

I worked out this recipe to make use of dried apricots. I have combined them with ground almonds to give a cake with a subtle flavour.

Cooking time: 50–60 minutes
Oven: 180°C, 350°F, Gas Mark 4
An 18 cm (7 in) square tin, 7.5 cm (3 in) deep, greased and base-lined

	METRIC	IMPERIAL
Dried apricots	115 g	4 oz
Granulated sugar	170 g	6 oz
Self-raising flour	340 g	12 oz
Ground almonds	70 g	2½ oz
A quarter of a grated nutmeg, or		
1 teaspoon (1 × 5 ml spoon) of		
ground nutmeg		
Soft margarine	115 g	4 oz
Honey	55 g	2 oz

100

2 eggs		
Milk	150 ml	¼ pint
Decoration:		
Apricot jam or apple jelly	115 g	4 oz
Split almonds	15 g	½ oz
A little angelica		

First chop the apricots finely, or if you have a liquidiser, put the sugar and the apricots in that and use maximum speed until the apricots are finely chopped. Sieve the flour into a mixing bowl. Stir in the ground almonds, grate in the nutmeg and tip in the chopped apricots and sugar. In a small saucepan gently warm the margarine and honey until melted. Cool a little, add the beaten eggs and milk and pour on to the flour mixture. Stir all together well. Pour into the prepared tin and bake in the centre of a moderate oven for 50–60 minutes, until the cake is just starting to shrink from the sides of the tin and the top is fairly firm. Leave to cool in the tin for 10 minutes, then turn out on a wire rack. Warm the sieved jam, brush it all over the cake, and arrange the almonds in threes to make flowers. Cut diamond-shaped leaves from the angelica. Decorate the whole top of the cake in this way.

To freeze: Store in a lidded container before brushing with jam.
To use: Thaw in container at room temperature for 5 hours. Then brush with jam or honey, or ice the cake.

Spicy Fruit Cake

I rather adore mixed spice in fruit cakes, so I really devised this recipe for people like me. Occasionally, I find there is a slice left for me!

Cooking time: 1½ hours
Oven: 170°C, 325°F, Gas Mark 3
A 19 cm (7½ in) round cake tin, greased and base-lined

101

	METRIC	IMPERIAL
Soft margarine	170 g	6 oz
Dark soft brown sugar	170 g	6 oz
3 eggs		
Orange marmalade	2 × 15 ml spoons	2 tablespoons
Plain flour	255 g	9 oz
Baking powder	1 × 5 ml spoon	1 teaspoon
Mixed spice	1 × 5 ml spoon	1 teaspoon
Ground nutmeg	1 × 5 ml spoon	1 teaspoon
Cinnamon	½ × 5 ml spoon	½ teaspoon
Mixed dried fruit	340 g	12 oz

Cream the margarine and sugar until light and fluffy. Gradually beat in the eggs and marmalade. Fold in the sifted flour, baking powder and spices alternately with the dried fruit. Spoon into the prepared tin, and bake in the centre of a very moderate oven for 1½ hours. Leave to cool in the tin for 10 minutes before turning out to cool on a wire rack. The cake will keep well for at least a week in a lidded container.

To freeze: Wrap or store in a box.
To use: Thaw in a container at room temperature for 5 hours.

Gooseberry Kuchen

This cake always evokes memories of childhood holidays in Germany. It is wonderful if eaten straight from the oven, and it is also delicious cold, with cream.

Cooking time: 50 minutes
Oven: 220°C, 425°F, Gas Mark 7, then turn down
A 20 cm (8 in) round tin, 2.5 cm (1 in) deep and well greased

	METRIC	IMPERIAL
Plain flour	115 g	4 oz
Baking powder	¼ × 5 ml spoon	¼ teaspoon
Caster sugar	30 g	1 oz
Soft margarine or butter	45 g	1½ oz
½ of an egg yolk		
Milk	1 × 15 ml spoon	1 tablespoon

Topping:

	METRIC	IMPERIAL
2 egg whites		
Caster sugar	85 g	3 oz
Ground almonds	55 g	2 oz
The finely grated rind of half a lemon		
Gooseberries, cooked and drained	340 g	12 oz
Cinnamon	¼ × 5 ml spoon	¼ teaspoon
Caster sugar	2 × 5 ml spoons	2 teaspoons

In a bowl sieve the flour and baking powder, stir in the sugar,
and cut in the butter or margarine until in very small pieces (rub
with fingertips if necessary). Mix to a dough with the egg yolk
and milk. Roll out the dough on a floured board to just over ½ cm
(¼ in) thick, and line the base and 2.5 cm (1 in) up the sides of the
tin with it. Now whisk the egg whites until really stiff, fold in half
the sugar, whisk again and then fold in the rest of the sugar, the
grated lemon rind and the ground almonds. Spoon the mixture
into the pastry case. Gently cover with the well-drained
gooseberries, and sprinkle with the caster sugar mixed with the
cinnamon. Bake in the centre of a hot oven for 15 minutes, and
then in a moderately hot oven for a further 35 minutes or until
the pastry is well cooked. Serve straight from the oven, or allow
to cool.

I don't freeze this kind of cake, since it is always nicer made just
before serving. It is equally good made with dark plums halved
on top, instead of gooseberries.

103

Fig and Lemon Cake

I make a green fig jam, and another from dried figs with lemon. This cake takes its cue from the second flavour, and it gives it a fruity, tangy taste which brings them back asking for more. We really like to eat it warm, about an hour after baking.

Cooking time: 1–1¼ hours
Oven: 180°C, 350°F, Gas Mark 4
An 18 cm (7 in) round cake tin, greased and base-lined

	METRIC	IMPERIAL
Dried figs (loose or packed)	170 g	6 oz
The finely grated rind of 1 lemon		
Soft margarine	170 g	6 oz
Light soft brown sugar	170 g	6 oz
3 eggs		
Wholewheat plain flour	85 g	3 oz
White plain flour	170 g	6 oz
Baking powder	1 × 5 ml spoon	1 teaspoon
Icing:		
Icing sugar	115 g	4 oz
Lemon juice	5–6 × 5 ml spoons	5–6 teaspoons
1 drop of yellow colouring		
Demerara sugar	1 × 5 ml spoon	1 teaspoon

Rinse the figs in warm water, cut off the stalks, and slice and chop them. Put in a bowl and pour 4 × 15 ml spoons (4 tablespoons) of boiling water over them. Stir in the grated lemon rind, keeping back ¼ × 5 ml spoon (¼ teaspoon) for the top of the cake. Leave to steep for 20 minutes. Cream the margarine and sugar until light and fluffy. Gradually beat in the eggs. Fold in the wholewheat flour, the sieved plain flour, the baking powder and the fig and lemon mixture. Turn into the prepared tin and bake in the centre of a moderate oven for 1–1¼ hours, until a skewer comes out cleanly from the cake. Leave in the tin for 10 minutes, then turn out to cool on a wire rack.

For the icing, sieve the sugar into a bowl, mix to a pouring consistency with the lemon juice, and add one drop of colouring to make it pale yellow. Pour on to the still warm cake. Mix the lemon rind you have kept back with the demerara sugar and sprinkle on the icing.

To freeze: Pack in a lidded box.
To use: Thaw in the container at room temperature for 4–5 hours.

GERALDENE HOLT'S CAKE STALL

TRAY-BAKED CAKES

This section is about one of the quickest ways of producing attractive home-baked cakes. At home I usually make two or three different kinds of tray-baked cakes or pastries at a time, pack a selection of squares into my cake tin and freeze all the rest in small packs. For the cake stall, it is very satisfying to be able to produce a good variety of cakes so quickly. If you need to turn out a lot of cakes in a short time — perhaps for a coffee morning, or for a bazaar or a fête — then this is the way to go about it. To sell them, arrange a selection on a pretty paper plate and cover with cling film.

Brownies

My mother is Canadian, and this is her recipe: tried and tested for forty years, and still just as popular. She insists that the glacé cherries are essential to give the moist yet crunchy bite that Brownies should have. The top is crisp and the inside sweetly fudgy.

Cooking time: 25–30 minutes
Oven: 180°C, 350°F, Gas Mark 4
A well-greased tray, 18 cm (7 in) square
Quantity: 16 brownies

	METRIC	IMPERIAL
Plain chocolate		
(eg Bourneville)	55 g	2 oz
White vegetable fat	55 g	2 oz
Caster sugar	115 g	4 oz
1 egg		
Vanilla essence	$\frac{1}{4}$ × 5 ml spoon	$\frac{1}{4}$ teaspoon
Plain flour	85 g	3 oz
Baking powder	$\frac{1}{4}$ × 5 ml spoon	$\frac{1}{4}$ teaspoon
Chopped walnuts	55 g	2 oz
Chopped glacé cherries	30 g	1 oz

Chop the walnuts, but not too finely. (I find the Zyliss round chopper excellent for nuts.) Chop the cherries. In a small saucepan gently heat the chocolate and fat. In a bowl, whisk the caster sugar and egg with a fork. Beat in the vanilla. Pour the melted chocolate and fat into the egg mixture, stirring with a spoon. Fold in the sieved flour and baking powder with the nuts and cherries. Pour into the baking tray and bake below the centre of a moderate oven (preferably just below another cake) for 25–30 minutes. A knife will come out clean when they are cooked. Cool in the tin for 15 minutes, then cut into sixteen pieces. Either leave in the tin until cold, or cool on a wire tray.

In Canada in the 1920s, each Brownie was wrapped separately

in paper and stored in a big cookie tin. I haven't tried this, since they all disappear so quickly; but they do freeze well.

To freeze: Store in lidded boxes or small plastic bags.
To use: Thaw in container at room temperature for 3 hours.

Iced Gingerbread

This is quite my best gingerbread recipe — just as good plain, but I find the cinnamon icing and glacé cherry decoration really make it scrumptious. And all that black treacle makes it good for you! This gingerbread has a light but moist texture.

Cooking time: 1¼ hours
Oven: 150°C, 300°F, Gas Mark 2
2 cake tins about 18 cm (7 in) square, or a deeper, larger one, greased and base-lined
Quantity: about 32 squares

	METRIC	IMPERIAL
Soft margarine	115 g	4 oz
Black treacle	170 g	6 oz
Golden syrup	55 g	2 oz
Milk	150 ml	¼ pint
2 eggs		
Plain flour	225 g	8 oz
Dark soft brown sugar	55 g	2 oz
Mixed spice	2 × 5 ml spoons	2 teaspoons
Ground ginger	3 × 5 ml spoons	3 teaspoons
Bicarbonate of soda	1 × 5 ml spoon	1 teaspoon
Icing:		
Icing sugar	225 g	8 oz
Ground cinnamon	¼ × 5 ml spoon	¼ teaspoon
The juice of half an orange		
Green and red glacé cherries, quartered, for decoration		

110

First sieve all the dry ingredients into a bowl. Then put a saucepan on the scales. Note its weight (write it down if you cannot remember figures) and then weigh the margarine, treacle and syrup into it. Gently heat the saucepan until the margarine has melted. Remove from heat, add the milk and leave to cool. Then add the beaten eggs. Pour this mixture on to all the dry ingredients in the bowl and stir well. Pour into the tins and bake in the centre of a slow oven for $1\frac{1}{4}$ hours. I always make it a golden rule never to peep at gingerbread while it is cooking for at least 40 minutes — otherwise it can sink in the middle. Turn out and cool on a wire tray.

For the icing, sieve the icing sugar and cinnamon into a bowl, add the orange juice and then just enough warm water to make a good pouring icing (not too thin). Pour over each slab of gingerbread. When set, mark into squares and decorate in a chessboard pattern with quartered glacé cherries placed diagonally on each square.

To freeze: Pack in a box, either plain or iced. Do not crush.
To use: Thaw in container at room temperature for 3 hours.

Sultana Slices

This is a tray-baked pastry with a delicious cinnamon and sultana filling. I usually use shortcrust pastry for this recipe although if you wish to add a little sugar, you could do so.

Cooking time: 35–40 minutes
Oven: 200°C, 400°F, Gas Mark 6
A swiss roll tin about 20 cm × 30 cm (8 in × 12 in), well greased
Quantity: 18 squares

	METRIC	IMPERIAL
Pastry:		
Plain flour	400 g	14 oz
A pinch of salt		
Soft margarine	100 g	3½ oz
White vegetable fat	100 g	3½ oz
Cold water	6 × 15 ml spoons	6 tablespoons
Filling:		
Soft margarine or butter	85 g	3 oz
Dark soft brown sugar	85 g	3 oz
Plain flour	1 × 15 ml spoon	1 tablespoon
Ground cinnamon	½ × 5 ml spoon	½ teaspoon
Honey	1 × 15 ml spoon	1 tablespoon
Sultanas	340 g	12 oz
For sugar crust:		
Milk	1 × 15 ml spoon	1 tablespoon
Caster sugar	1 × 15 ml spoon	1 tablespoon

For the pastry, use a knife to cut the fats into the flour and salt and then rub in using your fingertips. Mix to a dough with cold water, again using the knife. Put the ball of pastry into a plastic bag and then into the fridge to rest.

For the filling, gently heat the margarine, sugar, flour, cinnamon, honey and sultanas in a saucepan and allow to come to the boil. Continue to stir and thicken for 2 minutes. Remove from heat and allow to cool.

Divide the pastry in half. On a floured board roll out one half to fit into the base and sides of a swiss roll tin. Spread the filling over the pastry. Roll out the rest of the pastry and fit it over the top, gently pressing at the edges to ensure a good join. Brush the top of the pastry with the milk and sprinkle with caster sugar. Prick all over with a fork. Bake in a hot oven for 35–40 minutes until golden and crisp. Leave in the tin for 5 minutes, then cut into eighteen squares. Remove from tin when cool.

To freeze: Pack in sixes in plastic bags and store in a container.
To use: Thaw in bags at room temperature for 3 hours.

Chocolate Nut Slices

This is a variation I have devised of the sultana slice recipe. It is based on a delicious coffee bread which I can't resist when I'm in Germany.

Cooking time: 35 minutes
Oven: 200°C, 400°F, Gas Mark 6
A swiss roll tin about 20 cm × 30 cm (8 in × 12 in), greased
Quantity: 18 squares

	METRIC	IMPERIAL
Pastry:		
Plain flour	400 g	14 oz
A pinch of salt		
Soft margarine	100 g	3½ oz
White vegetable fat	100 g	3½ oz
Cold water	6 × 15 ml spoons	6 tablespoons
Filling:		
Soft margarine	85 g	3 oz
Light soft brown sugar	85 g	3 oz
Plain flour	1 × 15 ml spoon	1 tablespoon
Drinking chocolate	4 × 15 ml spoons	4 tablespoons

113

Chopped nuts	115 g	4 oz
Sugar crust:		
Milk	1 × 15 ml spoon	1 tablespoon
Caster sugar	1 × 15 ml spoon	1 tablespoon

Make the pastry by rubbing the fats into the flour until it is like breadcrumbs. Mix to a dough with the water and rest in the fridge. Make the filling by very gently heating the margarine, sugar, flour, drinking chocolate and nuts together. When thick and well combined, remove from heat and allow to cool.

Divide the pastry in half. Roll out one half on a floured board and use it to line the base and sides of the greased tin. Roll out the other half into a rectangle and, after spreading the filling, use it to cover. Dampen the edges and press together firmly. Brush milk over the top and sprinkle with caster sugar. Prick all over with a fork. Bake in a hot oven for 35 minutes. Cool for 5 minutes, then cut into squares or triangles. Remove from tin when cold.

To freeze: Pack in sixes in sealed plastic bags.
To use: Thaw in bags at room temperature for 3 hours.

Flapjack

So many people have told me of their problems with flapjack that I am including my favourite recipe for it. It is very important not to overcook it — don't be afraid to move its position in the oven while it is cooking. I use non-stick swiss roll tins for baking it, and I bake it until the sugar on the outside has caramelised into a crunchy toffee, while the centre is still moist and chewy. One of my best customers for this is my dentist and his family!

Cooking time: 30–35 minutes
Oven: 190°C, 375°F, Gas Mark 5
A swiss roll tin 23 cm × 30 cm (9 in × 12 in), or two smaller ones, very well greased
Quantity: About 24 pieces

	METRIC	IMPERIAL
Soft margarine	225 g	8 oz
Demerara sugar	170 g	6 oz
Golden syrup	55 g	2 oz
Rolled oats	290 g	10 oz
A pinch of salt		

Weigh the margarine, sugar and syrup directly into a good-sized saucepan. (Put the saucepan on the scales first and note its weight.) Gently heat until the margarine has melted. Remove from heat, stir well and add the rolled oats and salt. Use a spoon to mix it all together. Tip on to the greased tin and smooth level with the back of the spoon. Bake in a moderately hot oven for 30–35 minutes until the flapjack is quite golden at the edge of the tin. Leave to cool for 2 minutes, then with a sharp knife mark into twenty-four pieces. Leave to cool for at least 1 hour. Then cut through completely and remove with a flexible knife. (Keep any left-over crumbs for putting in treacle tarts.)

To freeze: Pack in sixes into small plastic bags.
To use: Thaw in bags at room temperature for 2 hours.

Lunch-Box Cake

This is one of the quickest fruit cakes to make. It has a lovely almond flavour and makes a good holiday cake. I always serve it cut into squares.

Cooking time: 1 hour
Oven: 170°C, 325°F, Gas Mark 3
2 tins measuring 25 cm × 15 cm (10 in × 6 in) and about 2.5 cm
(1 in) deep, well-greased
Quantity: 24 pieces

	METRIC	IMPERIAL
Soft margarine	225 g	8 oz
Caster sugar	225 g	8 oz
4 eggs		
Almond essence	$\frac{1}{2}$ × 5 ml spoon	$\frac{1}{2}$ teaspoon
Self-raising flour	285 g	10 oz
Mixed dried fruit	285 g	10 oz
Glacé cherries, quartered	85 g	3 oz
Chopped candied peel	55 g	2 oz
Granulated sugar	2 × 15 ml spoons	2 tablespoons

Cream the margarine and sugar until pale and fluffy. Gradually beat in the eggs and almond essence. Carefully fold in the sieved flour and also the fruit, until all are combined. Divide the mixture evenly between the two tins. Sprinkle granulated sugar over the top of the mixture in each tin. Bake them beside each other in the centre of a moderate oven. Leave in tin to cool, then cut into squares or rectangles before removing from tin.

To freeze: These cakes freeze splendidly, if packed into sealed plastic bags.
To use: Thaw in bags at room temperature for 3 hours.

Walnut and Lemon Cake

This quick-to-make cake has an unusual and appealing blend of flavours. You ice it in the tin, while still warm, and this is also a useful time-saver.

Cooking time: 45 minutes
Oven: 180°C, 350°F, Gas Mark 4
A 23 cm (9 in) square tin, well-greased
Quantity: 16 squares

	METRIC	IMPERIAL
Soft margarine	170 g	6 oz
Granulated sugar	170 g	6 oz
Self-raising flour	170 g	6 oz
Porridge oats	115 g	4 oz
Walnuts, chopped	45 g	1½ oz
The grated rind and juice of half a lemon		
2 large eggs		
Icing:		
Icing sugar	140 g	5 oz
The grated rind and juice of half a lemon		
2 drops of yellow food colouring		

Sieve the flour into a mixing bowl. Stir in the sugar, walnuts, lemon rind and oats. Use a knife to mix the margarine into the flour mixture. In a cup beat the eggs and lemon juice. Pour on to the mixture and stir together for 1 minute. Spoon into the well greased tin and spread evenly. Bake in the centre of a moderate oven for 45 minutes. Remove from the oven, leave in the tin and mix the sieved icing sugar with the other lemon juice and the colouring. Pour over the cake while it is warm and sprinkle with the grated lemon rind. Leave to cool and then cut into squares.

To freeze: The finished iced cake freezes very well. I pack the squares into a shallow plastic lidded box.
To use: Thaw in the container in a cool room for 3 hours. Do not remove the lid. otherwise warm air will condense into water on the cold icing.

Almond Triangles

These always go down well — a pastry-baked slice with a tasty almond macaroon top, blending crunchily with flaked almonds.

Cooking time: 25–30 minutes
Oven: 200°C, 400°F, Gas Mark 6
A tin measuring 25 cm × 15 cm (10 in × 6 in), greased
Quantity: 16 triangles

	METRIC	IMPERIAL
Pastry:		
Plain flour	225 g	8 oz
Soft margarine	55 g	2 oz
White vegetable fat	55 g	2 oz
1 egg yolk		
Cold water	3 × 15 ml spoons	3 tablespoons
Almond mixture:		
Caster sugar	115 g	4 oz
Icing sugar	115 g	4 oz
Ground almonds	115 g	4 oz
Ground rice	55 g	2 oz
1 whole egg		
1 egg white		
A few drops of almond essence		
A little apricot jam or apple jelly		
Flaked almonds	15 g	½ oz

Make the pastry by rubbing the fats into the flour, and mixing to a dough with the egg yolk and water. Rest the pastry. Mix the sugars, ground almonds and ground rice together. Stir in the beaten egg and white of egg, and the almond essence. Roll out the pastry on a floured board to fit the greased tin. Line the base and 1 cm (½ in) of the side of the tin with pastry. Spread apricot jam quite thinly over the pastry base. Carefully spoon the almond mixture over the jam. It's often easier to spread it with a

fork. Sprinkle the surface with flaked almonds and bake in the
centre of a hot oven for 25 minutes, then for 5 minutes on the
base of the oven to make the pastry base crisp. Leave to cool in
the tin, then cut into eight squares. Cut each of these diagonally
to give sixteen triangles.

To freeze: Almond triangles freeze perfectly, if packed in single layers
   in plastic bags, stored in a container.
To use: Thaw at room temperature for 3 hours in container.

Scotch Gingerbread

My son insists that I include this gingerbread recipe: it is his own
special favourite. The porridge oats and sultanas give it a moist,
crumbly texture — very satisfying in good big chunks.

Cooking time: 1–1¼ hours
Oven: 170°C, 325°F, Gas Mark 3
2 tins, each about 18 cm (7 in) square or a 25 cm (10 in) square tin,
greased and base-lined
Quantity: 18 squares

	METRIC	IMPERIAL
Soft margarine	170 g	6 oz
Black treacle	170 g	6 oz
Self-raising flour	170 g	6 oz
Rolled oats	170 g	6 oz
Light soft brown sugar	170 g	6 oz
Ground ginger	4 × 5 ml spoons	4 teaspoons
Ground cinnamon	2 × 5 ml spoons	2 teaspoons
Salt	1 × 5 ml spoon	1 teaspoon
Sultanas	170 g	6 oz
3 eggs		
Milk	275 ml	½ pint

Heat the margarine and treacle gently in a saucepan until the
margarine has melted. Remove from heat, and when cool stir in
the beaten eggs and milk. Sieve the flour and spices into a

good-sized bowl, and stir in the oats, sugar and sultanas. Pour in the treacle mixture and stir well. Pour into the lined and greased tin and bake in the centre of a moderate oven for 1–1¼ hours, until the cake is shrinking away slightly from the tin. Leave to cool in tin for 5 minutes, then remove and cool on wire rack. Serve cut into good-sized squares, and sprinkle the top with demerara sugar. All gingerbreads improve if kept for a day or two.

To freeze: Pack in container or in sealed plastic bags.
To use: Thaw in container at room temperature for 2 hours, then pop into a warm oven for 10 minutes to really bring out the flavour.

Cherry Walnut Slices

I make this in a rectangular non-stick tin for cutting, but it is just as nice baked in a round pie dish and served hot with cream for a pudding.

Cooking time: 35–40 minutes
Oven: 200°C, 400°F, Gas Mark 6
A tin 25 cm × 15 cm (10 in × 6 in) and 2.5 cm (1 in) deep, or 20 cm (8 in) diameter pie dish. Tin or dish must be well greased.
Quantity: 12 slices

	METRIC	IMPERIAL
Pastry:		
Plain flour	170 g	6 oz
Soft margarine	45 g	1½ oz
White vegetable fat	45 g	1½ oz
Cold water	3 × 15 ml spoons	3 tablespoons
Filling:		
Soft margarine	55 g	2 oz
Caster sugar	55 g	2 oz
1 large egg		

A few drops of vanilla essence		
Self-raising flour	85 g	3 oz
Glacé cherries (sliced)	55 g	2 oz
Chopped walnuts	55 g	2 oz
Cherry jam, or raspberry jam, or redcurrant jelly		
A little milk for mixing		
Granulated sugar for sprinkling		

Make the pastry by cutting the fats into the flour with a knife and then rubbing them in until like breadcrumbs. Mix to a soft dough with the water, using a knife. Rest the dough. Cream the margarine and sugar until fluffy, add the egg and vanilla essence. Gently fold in the sieved flour, cherries and walnuts with a little milk to give a very soft, dropping consistency. On a floured board roll out the pastry to fit the tin or dish, and spread the jam or jelly over the pastry base in a thin layer. Spread in the cherry walnut mixture and level off. Sprinkle with granulated sugar and bake in the centre of a hot oven for 35 minutes, then move to the base of the oven for 5 minutes to crisp the pastry base. Leave to cool in tin, then slice or serve hot.

To freeze: Pack slices in plastic bags.
To serve: Thaw at room temperature for 3 hours, or serve hot.

Orange Syrup Tart

This is another pudding recipe which I have adapted for use at tea-time. I much prefer it to the original treacle tart.

Cooking time: 30–40 minutes
Oven: 190°C, 375°F, Gas Mark 5
A non-stick tin 25 × 15 cm (10 in × 6 in), or a 20 cm (8 in) pie plate. Tin or plate must be greased
Quantity: 12 slices from the tin

	METRIC	IMPERIAL
Pastry:		
Plain flour	170 g	6 oz
Soft margarine	45 g	1½ oz
White vegetable fat	45 g	1½ oz
Cold water	3 × 15 ml spoons	3 tablespoons
Filling:		
2 large eggs		
The juice and rind of one orange		
Golden syrup	170 g	6 oz
A large handful of cornflakes		

Make the pastry by rubbing the fat into the flour until it resembles breadcrumbs. Mix to a dough with the water. Then beat the eggs with the grated rind and juice of the orange. Pour in the syrup and beat all together. On a floured board roll out the pastry to fit the base and run 1 cm (½ in) up the sides of the tin, or the base and sides of the pie dish. Pour the syrup filling into the lined tin. Sprinkle in one good handful of crushed cornflakes. Bake in the centre of a moderately hot oven for 35 minutes, and on the base of the oven for a further 5 minutes to crisp the pastry base. Leave to cool in tin before cutting into twelve slices.

To freeze: Pack in slices in a container.
To use: Thaw at room temperature for 2 hours.

Date Squares

This recipe has been a firm family favourite for many years, and is the kind of cake that's positively good for you!

Cooking time: 25–30 minutes
Oven: 180°C, 350°F, Gas Mark 4
A tin 28 cm × 18 cm (11 in × 7 in), well greased
Quantity: 15 squares

	METRIC	IMPERIAL
Oat crust:		
Soft margarine	115 g	4 oz
Self-raising flour	115 g	4 oz
Rolled oats	225 g	8 oz
Light soft brown sugar	115 g	4 oz
1 large egg		
Date filling:		
Stoned dates	225 g	8 oz
Cold water	4 × 15 ml spoons	4 tablespoons
Cornflour	1 × 5 ml spoon	1 teaspoon
A little milk		
Demerara or granulated sugar	1 ×15 ml spoon	1 tablespoon

With a knife cut the soft margarine into the flour, oats and sugar. Rub with the fingertips if necessary, until the margarine is well mixed. Mix to a dough with the beaten egg. On a floured board roll out half the dough to fit the base of the tin. Roll out the rest of the dough and leave on the board. Heat the dates with the water in a saucepan, and as they soften sprinkle the cornflour into the mixture and cook together until the mixture thickens. Cool for 5 minutes, with the occasional stir. Spread this over the oat crust base and gently place the rest of the rolled crust on top. Now brush the top with milk and sprinkle with demerara or granulated sugar. Prick with a fork. Bake in the centre of a moderate oven for 25–35 minutes. Leave in the tin to cool, but mark it out into squares straight away, using a sharp knife. Remove from tin when completely cold.

To freeze: Pack the squares into sealed plastic bags.
To use: Thaw at room temperature for 3 hours.

Cherry Shortbread

I usually make this near Christmas, when it's easier to buy the red, green and yellow glacé cherries which make the shortbread look so pretty. But you could use a mixture of red glacé cherries and chopped angelica at any time of the year.

Cooking time: 30 minutes
Oven: 170°C, 325°F, Gas Mark 3
2 non-stick baking tins 25 cm × 15 cm (10 in × 6 in), well-greased
Quantity: 18 fingers

	METRIC	IMPERIAL
Soft margarine or butter	225 g	8 oz
Caster sugar	170 g	6 oz
Almond essence	1 × 5 ml spoon	1 teaspoon
Plain flour	340 g	12 oz
Rice flour	115 g	4 oz
Glacé cherries (mainly red, but other colours too)	120–170 g	4–6 oz

In a warmed bowl cream the margarine and sugar until fluffy. Beat in the almond essence, then gradually add the sieved flours and chopped cherries. Combine until you can knead the mixture into one lump. Divide the mixture in two and then, with fingertips and the back of a spoon, press half of the mixture into each greased tin. Bake in the centre of a moderate oven for 30 minutes until it is changing to a golden colour at the edges. After 5 minutes, mark into fingers. Cut and remove from tin when cool.

To freeze: Pack in plastic bags.
To use: Thaw at room temperature for 2 hours.

Paradise Slices

I first discovered this pastry when a friend served it with morning coffee. It's really delicious, and very popular on the cake stall.

Cooking time: 35–40 minutes
Oven: 180°C, 350°F, Gas Mark 4
A baking tin, 28 cm × 18 cm (11 in × 7 in), well-greased
Quantity: 12 squares

	METRIC	IMPERIAL
Plain flour	170 g	6 oz
Soft margarine	45 g	1½ oz
White vegetable fat	45 g	1½ oz
Cold water	3 × 15 ml spoons	3 tablespoons
Filling:		
Soft margarine	115 g	4 oz
Caster sugar	115 g	4 oz
1 egg		
Ground almonds	30 g	1 oz
Ground rice	30 g	1 oz
Chopped cherries	55 g	2 oz
Chopped walnuts	45 g	1½ oz
Sultanas	170 g	6 oz
Apricot jam or apple jelly	1 × 15 ml spoon	1 tablespoon

First make the pastry by cutting the fats into the flour, rubbing in with fingertips and then mixing to a dough with water. Roll out on a floured board and line the base of the greased tin. Brush the pastry base with jam or jelly. Cream the margarine and sugar, beat in the egg, mix in the ground almonds and ground rice and then add the fruit and nuts. Spread the mixture carefully over the jam layer in the tin. Bake in the centre of a moderate oven for 35–40 minutes. Mark into fingers after 5 minutes. Cut through and remove from tin when completely cool. Dredge with icing sugar.

To freeze: Store in container. Do not crush the slices.
To use: Thaw at room temperature for 3 hours.

Chocolate Coconut Cake

This is a delicious single-layer cake, baked in a tray and cut into wedges. I find that even children who don't like coconut seem to like eating this!

Cooking time: 35–40 minutes
Oven: 180°C, 350°F, Gas Mark 4
A non-stick tin 28 cm × 18 cm (11 in × 7 in), greased
Quantity: 12 pieces

	METRIC	IMPERIAL
Soft margarine	115 g	4 oz
Caster sugar	115 g	4 oz
2 large eggs		
Self-raising flour	115 g	4 oz
Baking powder	$\frac{1}{4}$ × 5 ml spoon	$\frac{1}{4}$ teaspoon
Cocoa	2 × 15 ml spoons	2 tablespoons
Coconut	30 g	1 oz
Milk to mix		
Coating chocolate ('Scotbloc' plain is good)	115 g	4 oz

Cream together the margarine and sugar until light and fluffy. Beat in the eggs well. Sieve the flour, baking powder and cocoa together and gradually add to the egg mixture, along with the coconut and a little milk to mix. Spoon into a greased tin and bake in the centre of a moderate oven for 35–40 minutes, until the cake is beginning to shrink from the sides of the tin. Leave to cool in tin, and then pour the melted chocolate over the cake while it is still a little warm. Mark the top with the end of a round-bladed knife or the prongs of a fork. Cut in fingers when cold.

To freeze: Pack in small plastic bags.
To use: Thaw at room temperature for 3 hours.

Raspberry Almond Slices

I have read that in the view of the commercial bakeries, pastry-based cakes are the fastest-growing area in baking. So they are undeniably popular. Here is another good recipe, with a moist but crunchy texture, but not such a pronounced flavour as Almond Triangles.

Cooking time: 30–35 minutes
Oven: 180°C, 350°F, Gas Mark 4
A non-stick tin 28 cm × 18 cm (11 in × 7 in), greased
Quantity: 12 slices

	METRIC	IMPERIAL
Pastry:		
Plain flour	170 g	6 oz
Soft margarine	45 g	1½ oz
White vegetable fat	45 g	1½ oz
Cold water	3 × 15 ml spoons	3 tablespoons
Filling:		
Soft margarine	55 g	2 oz
Caster sugar	55 g	2 oz
1 large egg		
Almond essence	few drops	few drops
Self-raising flour	55 g	2 oz
Ground almonds	30 g	1 oz
Blanched flaked almonds	45 g	1½ oz
Milk to mix		
Raspberry jam	2 × 15 ml spoons	2 tablespoons

Make the pastry by rubbing the fats into the flour with the fingertips, and mixing to a dough with the water, using a knife. On a floured board roll out the pastry to fit the base and 1 cm (¼ in) up the side of the tin. Brush with raspberry jam. Cream the margarine and sugar until light and fluffy. Beat in the egg and almond essence. Fold in the sieved flour and ground almonds, and mix in a little milk to give a soft, spreading consistency. Spoon on to the jam surface with a teaspoon and spread evenly with a fork. Sprinkle the surface with flaked almonds. Bake in the centre of a moderately hot oven for 30 minutes. Leave to cool in tin. Cut into slices when cold.

To freeze: Pack in plastic bags or boxes.
To use: Thaw at room temperature for 3 hours. You could then warm it through in the oven and sprinkle with caster sugar.

Dutch Apple Cake

This batter-based cake with a fruit top is irresistible served hot with cream, but it's just as delicious cold. I rather like it at breakfast! It seems particularly good when made with Dutch butter.

Cooking time: 35–40 minutes
Oven: 200°C, 400°F, Gas Mark 6
A 20 cm (8 in) square tin, or 28 cm × 18 cm (11 in × 7 in) tin, well-greased
Quantity: 15 squares

	METRIC	IMPERIAL
Batter base:		
Butter	30 g	1 oz
Caster sugar	85 g	3 oz
1 egg, mixed with milk to make	150 ml	$\frac{1}{4}$ pint
Self-raising flour	170 g	6 oz
Baking powder	1 × 5 ml spoon	1 teaspoon
Grated lemon rind (optional)	1 × 5 ml spoon	1 teaspoon
Apple mixture:		
3–4 eating apples, medium size		
Granulated sugar	55 g	2 oz
Ground cinnamon	$\frac{1}{2}$ × 5 ml spoon	$\frac{1}{2}$ teaspoon
Ground nutmeg	$\frac{1}{4}$ × 5 ml spoon	$\frac{1}{4}$ teaspoon
Melted butter	30 g	1 oz

Cream the butter and caster sugar together in a bowl. Gradually add the egg and milk. Sieve the flour and baking powder into the bowl of mixture, add the lemon rind and beat together well for one minute. Pour this into the well-greased tin and brush the surface with the melted butter. In a small basin stir the spices into the granulated sugar. Peel, core and quarter the apples and slice thinly. Arrange them in overlapping rows on the butter and sprinkle the spiced sugar over the apple slices. Bake in a hot oven for 35–40 minutes. Either serve hot straight away or leave to cool in the tin and then cut into squares.

To freeze: Store in a plastic container.
To use: Thaw at room temperature for 3 hours.

Iced Fruit and Nut Squares

I always keep salted peanuts in the pantry — they are so useful as a snack, or for adding to winter salads; and I've worked out this recipe for a pastry-based sultana and peanut cake.

Cooking time: 30–35 minutes
Oven: 180°C, 350°F, Gas Mark 4
A non-stick baking tin 28 cm × 18 cm (11 in × 7 in), greased
Quantity: 12 squares

	METRIC	IMPERIAL
Pastry:		
Plain flour	170 g	6 oz
Soft margarine	45 g	1½ oz
White vegetable fat	45 g	1½ oz
Cold water	3 × 15 ml spoons	3 tablespoons
Filling:		
Soft margarine	55 g	2 oz
Caster sugar	55 g	2 oz
1 large egg		
A few drops of vanilla essence		
Self-raising flour	85 g	3 oz
Sultanas	85 g	3 oz

Chopped peanuts	45 g	1½ oz
Milk to mix		
Apricot jam or apple jelly	1 × 15 ml spoon	1 tablespoon
Icing:		
Icing sugar	55 g	2 oz
Hot water	1 × 15 ml spoon	1 tablespoon

For the pastry, rub the fats into the flour and mix to a dough with the cold water. Roll out to fit the base and 1 cm (¼ in) up the side of the tin. Brush the jam over the pastry. Now cream the margarine and sugar until light and fluffy, and beat in the egg and vanilla essence. Gently add the flour, and stir in the sultanas and nuts with a little milk to give a very soft consistency. Spoon this in little heaps on to the jam layer, and spread evenly with a fork. Bake in the centre of a moderate oven for 30 minutes, and move it to the base of the oven for a final 5 minutes. Leave to cool in tin, then mark into squares with a sharp knife. Mix the sieved icing sugar with the water, and trickle the icing from a dessertspoon in thin trails diagonally across the squares.

To freeze: Pack into containers or bags.
To use: Thaw at room temperature for 2 hours.

Quick-mix Chocolate Orange Cake

It's always useful to have an oil-based cake recipe for those times when you've nearly run out of margarine or butter. This recipe needs only 30 g (1 oz) of butter or margarine, and it's really quick to make. It eats well, too, with its crunchy topping.

Cooking time: 45 minutes
Oven: 190°C, 375°F, Gas Mark 5
An 18 cm (7 in) square tin, greased and lined
Quantity: 16 squares

	METRIC	IMPERIAL
Self-raising flour	140 g	5 oz
Cocoa	30 g	1 oz
Baking powder	1 × 5 ml spoon	1 teaspoon
Caster sugar	115 g	4 oz
The grated rind and juice of one orange		
2 eggs		
Corn oil	5 × 15 ml spoons	5 tablespoons
Milk	3 × 15 ml spoons	3 tablespoons
Icing:		
Honey	2 × 15 ml spoons	2 tablespoons
Butter or soft margarine	30 g	1 oz
Drinking chocolate	1 × 15 ml spoon	1 tablespoon
Crushed cornflakes	30 g	1 oz
Grated orange peel (kept back from above)	1 × 5 ml spoon	1 teaspoon

Sieve the flour, baking powder and cocoa into a bowl, stir in the sugar and grated orange rind (keeping 1 teaspoon back). Mix in the eggs with a fork. Add the orange juice, corn oil and milk and beat into the flour mixture until really smooth. Pour into the greased and lined tin and bake above the centre of a moderately hot oven until springy to the touch. Leave in tin for 5 minutes, then turn out to cool on a wire rack. For the icing, gently melt the butter (or margarine) and honey, and then stir in the drinking chocolate. When combined, add the crushed cornflakes and the orange rind. Spread over the warm cake. Allow to cool and cut into squares.

To freeze: Pack the squares into a plastic box.
To use: Thaw in container at room temperature for 2 hours.

Cherry Almond Meringue Fingers

If there's one egg left, this is a marvellous recipe for a quick tea-time treat. I use a rich short-crust pastry which forms an excellent base for any cake mixture, since it's more like short-bread.

Cooking time: 35–40 minutes
Oven: 180°C, 350°F, Gas Mark 4
A swiss roll tin, greased, 32 cm × 23 cm (13 in × 9 in)

	METRIC	IMPERIAL
Pastry:		
Self-raising flour	225 g	8 oz
Caster sugar	15 g	½ oz
Soft margarine	55 g	2 oz
White vegetable fat	55 g	2 oz
1 egg yolk		
Cold water	3 × 15 ml spoons	3 tablespoons
Meringue topping:		
1 egg white		
Icing sugar	115 g	4 oz
Flaked almonds	30 g	1 oz
Chopped glacé cherries	30 g	1 oz

Make the pastry by cutting the fats into the flour and sugar with a knife, then rubbing in with the fingertips until like fine bread-crumbs. Then mix to a dough with the egg yolk and water. Roll out on a floured board, and fit into the base and 1 cm (¼ in) up the side of the swiss roll tin. Whisk the egg white until slightly frothy. Tip in the sieved icing sugar and mix until well combined. Pour this sugar mixture on to the pastry base and sprinkle with the almonds and cherries. Bake in the centre of a moderate oven for 35 minutes, then move to the base of the oven for a final 5 minutes to crisp the pastry. Leave to cool in the tin for 10 minutes, then mark into fingers. Cut through and remove from tin when cool.

To freeze: Store in a container with minimum air included.
To use: Thaw in container at room temperature for 2 hours.

GERALDENE HOLT'S CAKE STALL

SMALL CAKES AND PASTRIES

Many people who are quite happy to bake a large fruit cake or gingerbread feel that individual cakes and pastries take too long to make. I hope to show in this chapter that, on the contrary, it's a very quick way to make cakes and that it can also prove to be very economical. Some small cakes, too, can only be made well at home. I hope you will discover some that are new and tempting.

Queen Cakes

These are the very British little fruit cakes which disappear so fast in my house or on the stall. I always use paper cases for these cakes — they seem to stay very fresh that way.

Cooking time: 15–20 minutes
Oven: 180°C, 350°F, Gas Mark 4
Bun or patty tins, lined with paper cases
Quantity: about 18 cakes

	METRIC	IMPERIAL
Soft margarine	115 g	4 oz
Caster sugar	115 g	4 oz
2 eggs, beaten		
Self-raising flour	170 g	6 oz
A pinch of salt		
A little finely-grated lemon or orange rind		
Currants	115 g	4 oz
Milk to mix		
A little granulated sugar for sprinkling		

Cream the margarine and sugar until light and fluffy. Gradually beat in the beaten eggs and grated rind, and add a little flour towards the end. Fold in half of the flour and salt, and then the remaining flour and the currants, together with a little milk to make a medium soft consistency. Spoon dessertspoonfuls of the mixture into the paper baking cases, making sure the cases are level in their tins. Sprinkle the surface of each cake with a little granulated sugar to give a sugar-crusted top. Bake in a moderate oven for 15–20 minutes, until well risen and golden in colour. Cool on a wire rack in their paper cases.

To freeze: Pack in lidded boxes or sealed bags.
To use: Thaw at room temperature for 2 hours in container.

Coffee Meringues

Meringues are a marvellous stand-by in the kitchen. Cooked at the end of a baking session in the dying heat of the oven, they can be stored for at least a month in an air-tight container (preferably on a high shelf in the kitchen, where the air is warmer). These meringues make an agreeable change from the usual plain ones; the coffee flavour counteracts the sugariness of the meringue. I usually put two meringues together with whipped cream and either serve them straight away, or put them in the freezer (or freezing compartment of the fridge) until ready to serve, to prevent the meringues softening.

Cooking time: 2 hours with oven on, then 1 hour to cool in oven
Oven: 100°C, 200°F, Gas Mark ¼
2 or 3 baking sheets, greased or lined with 'Bakewell' non-stick paper
Quantity: 12–18 sandwiched meringues

	METRIC	IMPERIAL
4 egg whites		
Caster sugar	115 g	4 oz
Granulated sugar	115 g	4 oz
Coffee essence	1 × 15 ml spoon	1 tablespoon

If you have problems making meringues, one trick worth using is to leave the egg whites in a cloth-covered bowl overnight at room temperature so that a little of the water in the egg whites evaporates. I certainly do this if I'm using very fresh eggs — it definitely helps.

Using a hand or electric egg whisk, beat the egg whites until they are firm and frothy. Gently add the caster sugar in three or four lots, beating well in between. Do the same with the granulated sugar, and then add the coffee essence in one trickle while beating gently — or add a small amount each time.

These days I usually pipe my meringues in the shape of a letter S, for serving plain or in a row of three or four blobs joined together for sandwiching. But for years I used a dessertspoon to drop blobs on to the baking sheet, and this works perfectly well. The above amount should give up to thirty-six small blobs on to two or three baking sheets. Bake them in a pre-heated oven, and after 1 hour gently change round the positions of the baking sheets so that you cook the meringues uniformly. After another hour turn off the oven and leave for at least a further hour — or overnight — to finish drying out. Gently remove them from the sheet and store them either as they are, or sandwiched with cream if they are about to be eaten or frozen.

Store the plain meringues in air-tight boxes, kept in a warm place.

Walnut Meringues

A Swedish friend gave me this recipe, and I have found it to be very popular. I sandwich the meringues with whipped cream, and sometimes, for a change, I flavour the cream with coffee or rum.

Cooking time: 2 hours with oven on, and at least 1 hour more with oven off
Oven: 100°C, 200°F, Gas Mark ¼
2–3 baking sheets, greased
Quantity: about 18 sandwiched meringues

	METRIC	IMPERIAL
4 egg whites		
Caster sugar	115 g	4 oz
Granulated sugar	115 g	4 oz
Finely-chopped walnuts	55 g	2 oz

Use the same method as for the coffee meringues. Gently fold in the chopped walnuts instead of the coffee essence.

Store in the same way as for coffee meringues.

137

Chocolate Cup Cakes

These little cakes are absolutely top of the pops with children, particularly if you decorate them with multi-coloured sweets (like Smarties) or chocolate drops. But there seem to be plenty of adults around who are addicted to them too. I always bake them in paper cases; children really adore peeling off the paper. I usually decorate them by pouring melted chocolate over them, and quickly sprinkle on the decoration before it sets.

Cooking time: 25 minutes
Oven: 180°C, 350°F, Gas Mark 4
Bun or patty tins lined with paper baking cases
Quantity: 18 cup cakes

	METRIC	IMPERIAL
Self-raising flour	115 g	4 oz
Baking powder	1 × 5 ml spoon	1 teaspoon
Caster sugar	115 g	4 oz
Soft margarine	115 g	4 oz
2 large eggs		
Cocoa	3 × 15 ml spoons	3 tablespoons
Hot water	2 × 15 ml spoons	2 tablespoons

Melted chocolate, and nuts or
sweets, for decoration

Put all the cake ingredients except the cocoa and water into a bowl. In a small basin mix the cocoa and hot water, immediately pour it on to all the other ingredients and mix all together very thoroughly. Beat for about 1 minute until it has a soft consistency. Place a dessertspoonful of mixture in each paper case. Bake in the centre of a moderate oven for 25 minutes, until the cakes are risen and firm. Cool on a wire tray.

To coat with melted chocolate, I usually replace the cakes in the patty tins so that they don't move as you spoon a good tea-spoonful of melted chocolate on to each one. Use the back of the spoon to help spread the chocolate if necessary. A gentle tap of the tin on the table will usually ensure the cakes are well coated. Immediately arrange halves of walnuts, split almonds or Smarties on the chocolate (possibly as two eyes, a nose and three for a mouth) before it sets.

To freeze: Pack in boxes.
To use: Thaw in container for 2–3 hours at room temperature, or overnight.

Almond Macaroons

Of all small cakes, these are my own personal favourite. I really do find them irresistible, perhaps because they are almost like a biscuit. I know people have problems removing them from the baking sheets. I usually use well-greased, non-stick baking sheets and remove them with a very thin flexible knife. If you still have problems, I suggest you use either rice paper or the excellent 'Bakewell' silicone paper which, if you are careful, can be used again.

Cooking time: 15 minutes
Oven: 190°C, 375°F, Gas Mark 5
2 baking sheets, well-greased or lined with rice paper or silicone paper
Quantity: 12 macaroons

	METRIC	IMPERIAL
2 egg whites		
Caster sugar	170 g	6 oz
Ground almonds	115 g	4 oz
Ground rice	30 g	1 oz
A few drops of almond essence		
12 split almonds		

139

Whisk the egg whites until stiff. Gently stir in half the sugar and whisk again. Then stir in all the rest of the ingredients. Mix well — the mixture should be quite stiff. Take a heaped tea-spoonful, roll it into a ball and gently press it down on to the prepared sheet or paper. Put six macaroons on each baking sheet, or more if you wish to make very small almond macaroons to use as petits fours or ratafias. Place a split almond on top of each macaroon. Bake in the centre of a moderate oven for 15–17 minutes until golden brown. Leave to cool for 5 minutes before removing and placing on wire tray.

To freeze: Pack in small plastic bags and seal.
To use: Thaw in container at room temperature for 2 hours.

Butter Tarts

This is one of my mother's Canadian recipes. The spicy fruit filling of these tarts makes them really delicious.

Cooking time: 20 minutes
Oven: 190°C, 375°F, Gas Mark 5
Bun or patty tins, well-greased
Quantity: 15 tarts

	METRIC	IMPERIAL
Shortcrust pastry:		
Plain flour	170 g	6 oz
Soft margarine	45 g	1½ oz
White vegetable fat	45 g	1½ oz
Cold water	2 × 15 ml spoons	2 tablespoons
Filling:		
Butter (or soft margarine)	55 g	2 oz
Dark soft brown sugar	55 g	2 oz
1 egg		
Ground cinnamon	½ × 5 ml spoon	½ teaspoon
Mixed spice	½ × 5 ml spoon	½ teaspoon
Currants	85 g	3 oz

For the pastry, rub the fats into the flour and mix to a dough with cold water. Leave to rest while making the filling.

Cream the butter and sugar. Beat in the egg, cinnamon, spice and currants. Now roll out the pastry until it is 3 mm ($\frac{1}{8}$ in) thick, cut out 7.5 cm (3 in) rounds and line the pastry tins for the individual tarts. Put a heaped teaspoonful of the filling into each one. Bake in the centre of a hot oven, and cook until the pastry is just changing colour. Turn out and cool on a wire tray.

To freeze: Pack carefully into plastic boxes.
To use: Thaw in container at room temperature for 1 hour.

New Zealand Kisses

This is a useful recipe to know about on those occasions when one runs out of eggs. These cakes have a good crunchy texture, with an unusual and tasty combination of dates and chocolate.

Cooking time: 15–20 minutes
Oven: 190°C, 375°F, Gas Mark 5
2 baking sheets, greased
Quantity: 16 finished kisses

	METRIC	IMPERIAL
Soft margarine	85 g	3 oz
Light soft brown sugar	85 g	3 oz
Plain flour	115 g	4 oz
Baking powder	1 × 5 ml spoon	1 teaspoon
Cocoa	1 × 15 ml spoon	1 tablespoon
A pinch of salt		A pinch of salt
Chopped walnuts	30 g	1 oz
Chopped dates	170 g	6 oz
Milk	1 × 15 ml spoon	1 tablespoon
Butter icing:		
Icing sugar	115 g	4 oz
Butter	55 g	2 oz
A little vanilla essence		

Cream the margarine and sugar until light and fluffy. Mix in the sieved flour, and the cocoa, baking powder and salt. Add the chopped walnuts, dates and milk, and mix well. Drop teaspoon-fuls on to the greased baking sheet and cook in a moderate oven for 15–20 minutes. Cool on a wire rack.

To make the butter icing, mix the sieved icing sugar with the softened butter and a few drops of vanilla essence, and add 1–2 teaspoons of milk if necessary to give a smooth cream. Use this to sandwich the kisses.

To freeze: Pack in bags or boxes.
To use: Thaw in boxes at room temperature for 1–2 hours.

Iced Coffee Cakes

These are delicious small afternoon cakes with a very soft texture, and coffee glacé icing topped with nuts. Again, I use paper cases for these because if you are batch baking, it means the tins can be used again straight away. And soft margarine enables you to get a very light mix.

Cooking time: 15–20 minutes
Oven: 180°C, 350°F, Gas Mark 4
Bun or patty tins, lined with paper cases
Quantity: 18 cakes

	METRIC	IMPERIAL
Soft margarine	115 g	4 oz
Caster sugar	115 g	4 oz
2 eggs, beaten		
A few drops of vanilla essence		
Self-raising flour	170 g	6 oz
A pinch of salt		
A little milk to mix		
Icing:		
Icing sugar	115 g	4 oz

142

Hot strong black coffee (made with coffee essence or powder)	1–2 × 15 ml spoons	1–2 tablespoons
Walnut halves, chopped or flaked nuts for decoration		

Cream the margarine and sugar until very light and fluffy. Gradually beat in the eggs and vanilla. Fold in the sifted flour and salt with a little milk, and make sure you haven't left uncombined margarine and sugar at the base of the bowl. Using a dessertspoon, spoon the mixture into eighteen cases. Bake just above the middle of a moderate oven until the cakes are well risen and golden. Cool on a wire rack.

For the icing, sieve the icing sugar into a bowl and mix with the hot coffee until the back of the spoon coats nicely with the glacé icing. Straight away, spoon the icing on to the cakes and coat each one. Decorate with chopped or flaked nuts, or with rosettes of butter cream.

To freeze: Pack in single layers in boxes.
To use: Thaw in container at room temperature for 2 hours.

Palmiers

Memories of Paris are revived whenever I make these crisp sweet pastries. They are just as delightful served plain or sandwiched with whipped cream. For speed I tend to use bought puff pastry and I find it gives a good result.

Cooking time: 15–20 minutes
Oven: 230°C, 450°F, Gas Mark 8
2 non-stick baking sheets, well-greased
Quantity: 10 sandwiched palmiers

	METRIC	IMPERIAL
Puff pastry	370 g	13 oz
Caster sugar	45 g	1½ oz
Whipping or double cream	150 ml	¼ pint
Vanilla sugar	1 × 15 ml spoon	1 tablespoon

First sprinkle your pastry board or working surface with a little caster sugar. Roll out the puff pastry to make an oblong 32 cm by 18 cm (13 in by 7 in) and sprinkle well with caster sugar. With the long side facing you, fold the left-hand edge to the centre of the pastry. Repeat with the right-hand edge of the pastry. Press down gently with the rolling-pin. Sprinkle with caster sugar and repeat the folding of the pastry by folding the sides into the centre to give four layers of pastry. Press gently together. Sprinkle with sugar and fold the two halves of folded pastry together to give eight layers. Using a sharp knife cut the folded pastry into twenty slices. Brush both sides of each slice with water and space six slices on a baking sheet. Sprinkle each slice with a little sugar and rest the sheet in the fridge for 10 minutes. Bake towards the top of a very hot oven for 15–20 minutes until golden brown. Leave to cool for 3 minutes then carefully remove with a flexible knife and cool on a wire rack.

Whip the cream until fairly stiff but still shiny, stir in the vanilla sugar (or use caster sugar and one drop of vanilla essence). Spoon on to half the palmiers and cover with the other halves.

To freeze: Pack single palmiers in a lidded container.
To use: Thaw in container at room temperature for 2 hours. Serve plain or sandwich with whipped cream.

Butterfly Cakes

These are pretty cakes for a birthday tea. If you have any differently coloured butter icing left over from other cakes, you can use it with these very effectively.

Cooking time: 15–20 minutes
Oven: 190°C, 375°F, Gas Mark 5
Bun or patty tins, lined with paper cases
Quantity: 15 cakes

	METRIC	IMPERIAL
Soft margarine	115 g	4 oz
Caster sugar	115 g	4 oz
2 eggs, beaten		
Self-raising flour	130 g	4½ oz
Butter icing:		
Icing sugar	115 g	4 oz
Butter	55 g	2 oz

A few drops of vanilla essence
(or other flavouring and colouring)

Cream the margarine and sugar until light and fluffy. Gradually beat in the eggs and add a little of the flour towards the end. Fold in the rest of the flour. Put dessertspoonfuls of the mixture into the paper cases and bake in the middle of a moderately hot oven for 15–20 minutes, until risen and golden. When the cakes are cool, cut a circle from the top of each cake. (I use a pointed, serrated vegetable knife for this.) Cut each circle in half to make wings.

To make the butter icing, cream the softened butter with the sieved icing sugar and flavouring. Spread a little butter cream on to the cake top. Gently press two wings on top of the cake at an angle, keep the straight sides of the wings adjacent. Pipe more butter cream between the wings and under each wing.

To freeze: Butterfly cakes can be frozen if packed carefully; but I prefer to freeze them whole without the icing, and ice the cakes before serving.

To use: Thaw at room temperature for 1–2 hours.

Lemon Drops

These little cakes are made by sandwiching two halves together. They have a fresh lemon tang — a little-used flavouring in cakes.

Cooking time: 15–20 minutes
Oven: 200°C, 400°F, Gas Mark 6
Baking sheets, greased
Quantity: 10 finished cakes

	METRIC	IMPERIAL
Self-raising flour	170 g	6 oz
Soft margarine	85 g	3 oz
Caster sugar	55 g	2 oz
The grated rind and juice of half a lemon		
1 large egg		
Granulated sugar	30 g	1 oz
Filling:		
Icing sugar	75 g	3 oz
Soft margarine	50 g	2 oz
A little lemon juice		
1–2 drops of yellow colouring		

Rub the margarine into the flour and sugar until the mixture is like breadcrumbs. Mix to a dough with the egg, beaten with the lemon juice and the grated rind. Divide the mixture into twenty pieces and roll each piece into a ball with a little granulated sugar in your hands. Place each ball on the baking sheet and flatten a little with a spoon. Bake in the centre of a hot oven for 15–20 minutes, until golden brown. Cool on a wire rack.

For the filling, mix the margarine into the icing sugar (sieved into a bowl), and add just enough lemon juice to give a soft, spreading icing. Colour it pale yellow with a few drops of yellow colouring. Pipe or spread the icing on to half the number of cakes, and then sandwich these with the others. Decorate by sprinkling with a very little sieved icing sugar.

To freeze: You can freeze the lemon drops either singly, or sandwiched with the filling. Pack them carefully into a lidded container.
To use: Thaw at room temperature for 2 hours.

Congress Tarts

These lovely little almond tarts seem always to be very popular. They look attractive when decorated with white glacé icing and a little piece of glacé cherry. I find they will keep in a tin for several days.

Cooking time: 20 minutes
Oven: 190°C, 375°F, Gas Mark 5
Bun or patty tins, greased
Quantity: 12 tarts

	METRIC	IMPERIAL
Pastry:		
Plain flour	170 g	6 oz
Margarine (or margarine mixed with white fat)	85 g	3 oz
Water	2 × 15 ml spoons	2 tablespoons
Filling:		
Caster sugar	85 g	3 oz
Butter	30 g	1 oz
1 egg		
A few drops of almond essence		
Ground rice	55 g	2 oz
Ground almonds	30 g	1 oz
A little raspberry or strawberry jam		
Icing sugar	50 g	2 oz
Hot water	1 × 15 ml spoon	1 tablespoon
Glacé cherries for decoration		

For the pastry, rub the margarine or mixed fats into the flour until the mixture resembles fine breadcrumbs. Mix to a dough with the water, using a knife. Gently knead the mixture in the bowl until the pastry is in one piece. Leave to rest. For the filling, mix the sugar and butter with a fork. Add the lightly beaten egg and almond essence, and beat well until smooth. Fold in the ground rice and ground almonds. Roll out the pastry on a floured board until 3 mm ($\frac{1}{8}$ in) thick. Cut 7.5 cm (3 in) rounds and line the greased patty tins with them. Place a coffeespoonful of jam in the base of each tart and cover with a heaped tea-spoonful of the almond filling. Bake in a hot oven for 20 minutes. Cool in the tin or on a wire rack, and then spoon over each tart some glacé icing made by mixing the sieved icing sugar with a tablespoon of hot water. Place a quarter of a glacé cherry on top of each tart.

To freeze: Pack in single layers in containers. I prefer to freeze them plain and ice after thawing.
To use: Thaw very slowly for 3–4 hours in a cool room.

Coffee or Chocolate Éclairs

Home-made éclairs filled with whipped cream and shining with coffee glacé icing or melted chocolate just cannot be bettered anywhere. Make these as a treat or a celebration. They are made from choux pastry, which is not difficult; but to make finger éclairs it is necessary to pipe the mixture. If you prefer, use a spoon instead and make cream puffs or tiny profiteroles, to be served with chocolate sauce or caramel.

Cooking time: 30 minutes
Oven: 220°C, 425°F, Gas Mark 7
2 baking trays, well-greased
Quantity: 12 éclairs

	METRIC	IMPERIAL
Boiling water	150 ml	$\frac{1}{4}$ pint
Soft margarine	55 g	2 oz
Plain flour	85 g	3 oz
A pinch of salt		
2 eggs		
Double cream	275 ml	$\frac{1}{2}$ pint

148

Vanilla sugar	1×15 ml spoon	1 tablespoon
Coffee icing:		
Icing sugar	170 g	6 oz
Instant coffee powder	1×15 ml spoon	1 tablespoon
Hot water	6×5 ml spoons	6 teaspoons

Sieve the flour and salt on to a piece of greaseproof paper. Measure the boiling water into a saucepan. Add the margarine in small lumps and stir until it has melted. Bring the liquid to the boil. Remove from heat and add the flour and salt. Beat over moderate heat for a few minutes until the paste forms a ball and leaves the sides of the saucepan. Remove from heat. Crack the eggs into a cup and break with a fork. Gradually beat the eggs into the paste, making sure each addition is well combined. Now beat the mixture for 1 minute, until smooth and glossy. Spoon the mixture into a cotton or nylon piping bag fitted with a plain 1 cm ($\frac{1}{2}$ in) nozzle. Pipe six éclairs on to each baking sheet, each about 7.5 cm (3 in) long, or spoon twelve neat heaps on to the baking trays. Bake above the centre of a hot oven for 10 minutes, then carefully move one tray to the centre of the oven for a further 20 minutes, keeping the other tray above the centre of the oven. Remove from oven when golden and crisp. Immediately pierce the side of each éclair with a sharp knife to allow steam to escape, and rest them, cut side uppermost, on a wire rack.

Whip the cream with a little vanilla sugar until thick and glossy. Make a long incision on one side of each cooled éclair. Pipe cream into each one. For the icing, dissolve the coffee in the hot water in a small bowl. Add the sieved icing sugar and mix to a pouring consistency. Spoon over the éclairs, and leave to set. Or, instead of coffee icing, melt some chocolate and coat the éclairs with it.

I think éclairs are really best eaten freshly-made, but they will freeze.

To freeze: Store in a lidded container.
To use: Thaw in container in a cool room for 3 hours.

Ginger Hats

These are small ginger cakes with cinnamon icing, made to look like hats. They are a good choice for a cake stall because they are unusual.

Cooking time: 15 minutes
Oven: 190°C, 375°F, Gas Mark 5
Bun or patty tins, well-greased
Quantity: 18 hats

	METRIC	IMPERIAL
Soft margarine	115 g	4 oz
Dark soft brown sugar	55 g	2 oz
Treacle	55 g	2 oz
2 eggs		
Self-raising flour	170 g	6 oz
Ginger	1 × 5 ml spoon	1 teaspoon
Mixed spice	1 × 5 ml spoon	1 teaspoon
Coffee powder	1 × 5 ml spoon	1 teaspoon
Icing:		
Icing sugar	115 g	4 oz
Unsalted butter	45 g	$1\frac{1}{2}$ oz
Cinnamon	$\frac{1}{4}$ × 5 ml spoon	$\frac{1}{4}$ teaspoon
Milk	1 × 5 ml spoon	1 teaspoon

Cream the margarine, sugar and treacle until well combined and fluffy. Gradually beat in the eggs, with a little flour added towards the end. Mix in the rest of the sifted flour and spices, and coffee powder and beat for half a minute. Put rounded

150

dessertspoonfuls into the well-greased patty tins. Bake just above the centre of a moderate oven for 15 minutes. Cool in tins for 3 minutes, then lift out on to a wire rack. Sieve the icing sugar into a bowl and mix in the butter with a fork. Add the cinnamon and beat to a smooth cream with the milk if necessary. Spoon the icing into a piping bag or tube with a star-shaped nozzle. Using a sharp, pointed knife held vertically, cut away a circle from the top of each cake and lift out — this will form the crown of the hat. Pipe the butter icing around the edge of the hole, plus a little in the dip. Replace the circle of cake and press down very gently. If you wish you can spread the icing — but piping does look prettier.

To freeze: Pack in single layers in lidded boxes.
To use: Thaw at room temperature in container for 2 hours.

Japonnais Cakes

This version of these tempting little cakes is easier to make than the traditional one, Use hazelnuts complete in their brown skins. I find a liquidiser is excellent for grinding these but in some health food shops you may find them already ground.

Cooking time: 30 minutes
Oven: 160°C, 325°F, Gas Mark 3
2 baking sheets, lined with lightly-oiled 'Bakewell' cooking paper
Quantity: 12 sandwiched cakes

	METRIC	IMPERIAL
2 egg whites		
Caster sugar	115 g	4 oz
Ground hazelnuts	55 g	2 oz
Cornflour	1 × 15 ml spoon	1 tablespoon
Icing:		
Icing sugar	115 g	4 oz
Unsalted butter	85 g	3 oz
Coffee essence to flavour		

151

Whisk the egg whites until stiff. Whisk in half the sugar, and continue whisking until stiff again. Fold in the rest of the sugar and then the ground hazelnuts and cornflour, mixed together. When well combined, use a dessertspoon to place twelve spoonfuls on each baking sheet. Bake in the centre of a very moderate oven for 30 minutes. Then lift them gently from the paper and set to cool on a wire rack.

Make the butter icing by creaming the butter with the sieved icing sugar. Beat in a little coffee essence until of the right strength. Sandwich the cakes with the icing. A little melted chocolate can be poured on top of each one, if desired.

To freeze: Store the cakes in a lidded container without sandwiching them.
To use: Thaw in container at room temperature for 1 hour, then sandwich with butter icing and decorate.

Mince Pies

At home I make mince pies only in December, but I discovered on the cake stall that they are popular nearly all the year round. I think the pastry should be light and short, and they are always improved by a thin sugar crust. For a Christmas party I make mince pies with a star shape cut away from the lid, and I pour brandy or rum through this just before serving hot. I finish off by dusting them with icing sugar.

Cooking time: 20 minutes
Oven: 200°C, 400°F, Gas Mark 6
Patty tins, greased
Quantity: 12 pies

	METRIC	IMPERIAL
Plain flour	225 g	8 oz
A pinch of salt		
Soft margarine	55 g	2 oz
White vegetable fat	55 g	2 oz
Water	4 × 15 ml spoons	4 tablespoons
Mincemeat	225 g	8 oz
A little milk		
Granulated sugar for sprinkling		

Sift the flour and salt into a bowl. Put the margarine and fat in the bowl and, with a knife, cut into little pieces. Use your fingertips to rub the fat into the flour until the mixture resembles breadcrumbs. Mix to a soft dough with the water. If you now have time to rest the pastry for 5–10 minutes, the gluten will be released from the flour and this will make it easier to handle. On a floured board roll out half the pastry to 3 mm ($\frac{1}{8}$ in) thickness. With a 7.5 cm (3 in) fluted cutter make twelve circles. Line the patty tins with these. Put about one well-rounded dessertspoon-ful of mincemeat into each pastry case. Roll out the rest of the pastry and cut another twelve circles, but this time use a 6.5 cm ($2\frac{1}{2}$ in) fluted cutter. Brush milk over the underside of each lid and press gently on to the mincemeat, making sure you have placed it centrally. Brush the top with milk and sprinkle with granulated sugar. Bake above the centre of a moderately hot oven for 20 minutes. Cool in the tin for 10 minutes, then lift out on to a wire rack.

If you use commercially-made mincemeat, it is much improved by stirring into it finely grated orange or lemon rind, and some mixed spice.

To freeze: Mince pies freeze perfectly. Pack them carefully in lidded containers.
To use: Thaw in container at room temperature for 3 hours. Then warm through in oven.

Coconut Macaroons

I have experimented with a great many coconut macaroon recipes over the years, and after much adapting I am happy with this one.

Cooking time: 20–25 minutes
Oven: 180°C, 350°F, Gas Mark 4
2 or 3 non-stick baking sheets, well-greased
Quantity: about 24 macaroons

	METRIC	IMPERIAL
4 egg whites		
Caster sugar	140 g	5 oz
Granulated sugar	140 g	5 oz
Desiccated coconut	225 g	8 oz
Cornflour	30 g	1 oz

Whisk the egg whites until stiff. Gradually add the caster sugar, whisking between each addition. Fold in the granulated sugar, the coconut and the cornflour.

Spoon the mixture into small heaps on the baking sheets and bake in a moderate oven for 20–25 minutes. Gently exchange the positions of the baking sheets during cooking, to ensure even cooking. Leave to cool on trays for 5 minutes, then gently lift off the macaroons with a knife and cool on a wire rack. Some people in Devon are naughty enough to sandwich them with clotted cream!

To freeze: Pack in boxes.
To use: Thaw in container at room temperature for 1 hour. Use within a few days, because coconut can develop an off-flavour if it gets stale.

GERALDENE HOLT'S CAKE STALL

BISCUITS AND COOKIES

This is a vastly under-rated area of home cooking. Not only do home-made biscuits taste much better than the factory ones — they really are a money-saver. I find that biscuits disappear in a flash from the cake stall. They are useful because they store so well, kept in an air-tight jar or plastic container. And I find, too, that they freeze perfectly for up to six months — which came as rather a surprise to me. Without doubt, there is plenty of scope for you to run a stall selling nothing but home-made biscuits — you'd never have any left over. I have included a big selection of biscuit and cookie recipes because' they are all so popular. I hope you will soon find your own favourites among them.

Biscuits and cookies fall into two distinct groups. There are the rolled out and cut ones (which mainly covers the biscuits), and those (mainly the cookies) which you make by dropping the mixture from a spoon on to a baking tray, or which you shape in your hand first. The second group are amazingly quick to make, .but the enjoyment of making those in the first group more than compensates for the slightly longer working method. Both sorts taste good!

The other wonderful advantage of making biscuits and cookies is that you need so little in the way of kitchen equipment. A bowl, a knife, fork and spoon and a baking tray — and you're there. I prefer well-greased non-stick baking trays now, but I managed perfectly well for years before non-stick coatings were invented.

Coconut Syrup Biscuits

These are crisp and nutty — just what everyone seems to like.

Cooking time: 10 minutes
Oven: 180°C, 350°F, Gas Mark 4
A baking tray, well-greased
Quantity: about 25 biscuits

	METRIC	IMPERIAL
Plain flour	115 g	4 oz
Light soft brown sugar	85 g	3 oz
Soft margarine	55 g	2 oz
Desiccated coconut	115 g	4 oz
Bicarbonate of soda	$1\frac{1}{2}$ × 5 ml spoons	$1\frac{1}{2}$ teaspoons
Golden syrup	85 g	3 oz

Rub the margarine into the flour and sugar. Add the other ingredients and bind together using a fork. Form dessertspoonfuls of the mixture into balls, flatten them slightly and place on the baking tray. Bake in a moderate oven for 10–15 minutes. Leave to cool on a wire tray.

To freeze: Pack them in tens in small plastic bags, and store in a closed container.
To use: Leave to thaw for 1 hour at room temperature.

Orange Nut Drop Cookies

These cookies really are so quick to make — and I don't know of any commercially-baked biscuit which approaches them for flavour.

Cooking time: 12 minutes
Oven: 190°C, 375°F, Gas Mark 5
A baking tray, greased
Quantity: about 30 cookies

	METRIC	IMPERIAL
Soft margarine	115 g	4 oz
Caster sugar	85 g	3 oz
Light soft brown sugar	30 g	1 oz
2 egg yolks (or 1 whole egg)		
The grated rind and juice of one orange		
Plain flour	140 g	5 oz
Bicarbonate of soda	½ × 5 ml spoon	½ teaspoon
Finely chopped salted peanuts	45 g	1½ oz

Cream the margarine and sugar until fluffy. Mix in the egg yolks (or egg), and the orange rind and orange juice. Stir in the flour and bicarbonate. When well combined, add the nuts. Drop heaped teaspoons of the mixture on to a greased baking tray. Space them well, to allow for spreading. Bake in a moderately hot oven for about 12 minutes until golden. Remove from oven, and gently lift the cookies off the tray with a flexible knife. The cookies will become crisp as they cool on the wire rack.

To freeze: Pack into small plastic bags and store in a closed container.
To use: Leave to thaw in their bag at room temperature for 1 hour.

Chocolate Nut Drop Cookies

This is a variation on the previous recipe, and every bite as good.

Cooking time: 12 minutes
Oven: 190°C, 375°F, Gas Mark 5
A baking tray, greased
Quantity: about 30 cookies

	METRIC	IMPERIAL
Soft margarine	115 g	4 oz
Caster sugar	55 g	2 oz
Soft brown sugar	55 g	2 oz

2 egg yolks (or 1 whole egg)

Plain flour	140 g	5 oz
Bicarbonate of soda	$\frac{1}{2}$ × 5 ml spoon	$\frac{1}{2}$ teaspoon
Plain chocolate (finely chopped)	45 g	$1\frac{1}{2}$ oz
Walnuts (finely chopped)	45 g	$1\frac{1}{2}$ oz

Follow the same method as in the previous recipe.

To freeze: Pack in tens in plastic bags, and store in a closed container.
To use: Leave to thaw in their bag at room temperature for 1 hour.

Easter Biscuits

These biscuits make an attractive present, wrapped in tissue paper and tied with ribbon. Older people living alone appreciate them — a home-made biscuit is often a treat for them. The spicy taste of these biscuits makes them one of my own favourites.

Cooking time: 15 minutes
Oven: 180°C, 350°F, Gas Mark 4
A baking tray, greased
Quantity: about 20 biscuits

	METRIC	IMPERIAL
Soft margarine	115 g	4 oz
Caster sugar	115 g	4 oz
1 small egg		
Plain flour	225 g	8 oz
Mixed spice	1 × 5 ml spoon	1 teaspoon
Currants	55 g	2 oz
A little beaten egg white, or milk		
Granulated sugar for sprinkling		

Cream the margarine and sugar, and beat in the egg. Gradually work in the rest of the ingredients, and then knead lightly with the fingertips to give a soft dough. Roll out the dough on a floured board to just under ½ cm (¼ in) thick. Then use a 7.5 cm (3 in) fluted cutter to form the biscuits. Place the biscuits on the greased baking tray, and brush them gently with beaten egg white or milk. Sprinkle them with granulated sugar. Bake for about 15 minutes, until the biscuits are a pale gold. Leave them to cool for a few minutes before removing them from the tray and allowing to cool on a wire rack.

To freeze: Pack them in tens in plastic bags, and store in a closed container.
To use: Allow to thaw at room temperature for 1 hour.

Chocolate Crunch Cookies

I know of one family where the children will eat no other biscuits but these. They do have a very more-ish flavour.

Cooking time: 15 minutes
Oven: 170°C, 325°F, Gas Mark 3
A baking tray, greased
Quantity: about 24 cookies

	METRIC	IMPERIAL
Soft margarine	170 g	6 oz
Light brown sugar	115 g	4 oz
Self-raising flour	225 g	8 oz
Cocoa	2 × 15 ml spoons	2 tablespoons
Crushed cornflakes	55 g	2 oz
A pinch of salt		
A few drops of vanilla essence		
Melted chocolate and flaked or chopped almonds for decoration		

Cream the margarine and sugar. Beat in the cocoa, salt, vanilla and then gradually stir in the flour and cornflakes until all are

160

completely combined. Shape teaspoonfuls of the mixture into balls, flatten them a little and place them on greased baking trays (they spread a little in cooking). Bake in a moderate oven for 15 minutes until just firm. When cool, spoon a little melted chocolate into the centre of each cookie and sprinkle nuts on the top.

To freeze: Pack them in tens in plastic bags and then store in a closed container.
To use: Leave to thaw at room temperature for 1 hour.

Shortbread Biscuits

These are my all-time favourite. I always use unsalted butter for shortbread, and everyone seems to appreciate the subtle flavour it imparts.

Cooking time: 20 minutes
Oven: 170°C, 325°F, Gas Mark 3
A baking tray, greased
Quantity: about 20 biscuits

	METRIC	IMPERIAL
Unsalted butter	115 g	4 oz
Caster sugar	55 g	2 oz
Plain flour	170 g	6 oz

First warm the mixing bowl by pouring hot water in and out of it, or by leaving the bowl in a really warm place for half an hour. Now put the butter in the bowl, and beat well with a wooden spoon or fork until very soft. Add the sugar, and cream both together. Gradually add the flour, and continue beating until the whole mixture binds together into a ball. On a floured board and with a floured rolling-pin, roll out the mixture until it is $\frac{1}{2}$ cm ($\frac{1}{4}$ in) thick. Cut rounds from it with a 6 cm ($2\frac{1}{2}$ in) or 7.5 cm (3 in)

161

fluted cutter. Gently place on the greased baking trays and prick each biscuit with a fork. Bake in a slow oven for 20 minutes, until just changing colour at the edges. Cool on a wire rack and sprinkle with caster sugar.

To freeze: Pack in small sealed plastic bags in a container.
To use: Thaw in bags at room temperature for 1 hour.

Anzacs

I was given this recipe years ago by an Australian friend. These are very nutritious biscuits — they really seem to satisfy ravenous children.

Cooking time: 15–20 minutes
Oven: 170°C, 325°F, Gas Mark 3
A baking tray, greased
Quantity: about 30 biscuits

	METRIC	IMPERIAL
Plain flour	115 g	4 oz
Rolled oats	115 g	4 oz
Desiccated coconut	115 g	4 oz
Soft dark brown sugar	115 g	4 oz
Baking powder	$\frac{1}{2}$ × 5 ml spoon	$\frac{1}{2}$ teaspoon
Soft margarine	115 g	4 oz
Golden syrup	2 × 15 ml spoons	2 tablespoons
Water	2 × 15 ml spoons	2 tablespoons

Mix all the dry ingredients together in a bowl. In a saucepan, heat gently the margarine, syrup and water. Pour this into the bowl and with a spoon mix everything well together. Roll teaspoons of the mixture into small balls, flatten them and place on the prepared tray. Bake in a very moderate oven for 15–20 minutes. Leave them on the tray to cool for 2 minutes, then allow to cool on a wire rack.

To freeze: Pack in tens in plastic bags.
To use: Thaw in bag at room temperature for 1 hour.

Ginger Nuts

There is something about the intense flavour of a home-baked ginger nut which makes them quite irresistible. And they are so easy! One of the quickest puddings ever can be made by sandwiching the ginger nuts with whipped cream and serving them with chocolate sauce.

Cooking time: 15–20 minutes
Oven: 170°C, 325°F, Gas Mark 3
A baking tray, greased
Quantity: 40 biscuits

	METRIC	IMPERIAL
Self-raising flour	225 g	8 oz
Caster sugar	115 g	4 oz
Ground ginger	2 × 5 ml spoons	2 teaspoons
Bicarbonate of soda	1 × 5 ml spoon	1 teaspoon
Golden syrup	2 × 15 ml spoons	2 tablespoons
Black treacle	2 × 15 ml spoons	2 tablespoons
Soft margarine	85 g	3 oz
1 egg		

Sieve all the dry ingredients together into a bowl. Measure the syrup, treacle and margarine into a saucepan and heat gently until melted. Remove from heat and add the beaten egg. Then pour this on to the flour mixture in the bowl and beat well.

163

Leave to cool slightly. Form heaped teaspoonfuls into balls, and then place them — spaced well apart — on the baking trays. Bake in a very moderate oven for 15–20 minutes. Leave to cool for a few minutes before removing the biscuits from the tray with a flexible knife. Allow to cool on a wire rack.

To freeze: Pack them in tens in well-sealed plastic bags, to ensure the ginger flavour is retained.
To use: Leave to thaw in the bag at room temperature for 1 hour.

Fairy Rings

I devised these crunchy vanilla biscuits as an accompaniment to home-made yoghourt; but they are just as nice on their own.

Cooking time: 12–15 minutes
Oven: 180°C, 350°F, Gas Mark 4
A baking tray, greased
Quantity: about 20 rings

	METRIC	IMPERIAL
Plain flour	225 g	8 oz
Caster sugar	115 g	4 oz
Soft margarine	115 g	4 oz
2 egg yolks		
Vanilla essence	$\frac{1}{2}$ × 5 ml spoon	$\frac{1}{2}$ teaspoon
Top of milk	2 × 15 ml spoons	2 tablespoons
Demerara sugar	1 × 15 ml spoon	1 tablespoon

Rub the margarine into the flour and the sugar until the mixture is like breadcrumbs. Beat the egg yolks, 1 tablespoon of top of milk and vanilla together and add this to the dry ingredients. Stir well to make a soft dough. On a floured board roll out to 3 mm ($\frac{1}{8}$ in), and then use a 7.5 cm (3 in) fluted cutter to cut out the biscuits. Use a 2.5 cm (1 in) fluted cutter to remove the centre of

164

each biscuit. Place them on the prepared baking tray, brush each one gently with a little more top of milk (or egg yolk) and then sprinkle each one with demerara sugar. Bake towards the top of a moderate oven for 12–15 minutes until golden. Remove from the oven, lift the biscuits on to a wire rack and leave to cool.

To freeze: Pack in tens in sealed plastic bags.
To use: Thaw at room temperature for 1 hour.

Chocolate Chews

These have a crisp, chocolatey taste. This is a good recipe for using up the whites of egg left over from the Fairy Rings recipe.

Cooking time: 12–15 minutes
Oven: 180°C, 350°F, Gas Mark 4
A baking tray, well-greased
Quantity: about 24 chews

	METRIC	IMPERIAL
2 egg whites		
Granulated sugar	30 g	1 oz
Caster sugar	115 g	4 oz
Drinking chocolate	55 g	2 oz
Crushed cornflakes	115 g	4 oz
Rolled oats	30 g	1 oz
Chopped candied peel	30 g	1 oz
Coffee essence	1 × 5 ml spoon	1 teaspoon

Whisk the egg whites until stiff and in peaks. Add the granulated sugar and beat again. Continue to whisk gradually, adding spoonfuls of the caster sugar and drinking chocolate previously mixed together in a cup. Remove the whisk and add the crushed cornflakes oats, peel and coffee. Stir until combined.

165

Now take a dessertspoonful of this mixture at a time, and make piles on the prepared tray. Bake for 12–15 minutes in a moderate oven. Cool on a wire rack. The chocolate chews can be decorated with melted chocolate if you wish.

To freeze: Pack in a container or box.
To use: Thaw in container at room temperature for 1 hour.

Butterscotch Biscuits

I discovered this recipe in a cookery book dating from the 1920s. I like to serve these unusual biscuits with vanilla or rum ice cream. They always disappear very fast on the cake stall. You must remember, though, to rest the mixture for an hour in a cold place.

Cooking time: 8–10 minutes
Oven: 180°C, 350°F, Gas Mark 4
A baking tray, greased
Quantity: about 24 biscuits

	METRIC	IMPERIAL
Butter	55 g	2 oz
Golden syrup	170 g	6 oz
Vanilla essence	$\frac{1}{2}$ × 5 ml spoon	$\frac{1}{2}$ teaspoon
Bicarbonate of soda	$\frac{1}{2}$ × 5 ml spoon	$\frac{1}{2}$ teaspoon
Self-raising flour	170 g	6 oz
Walnuts or flaked almonds	30 g	1 oz

Melt the butter and syrup in a saucepan. Remove from heat and add vanilla and bicarbonate of soda. Stir well. Pour this on to the sieved flour, mix thoroughly and leave in a bowl to get really cold — preferably in the fridge. (It takes less time if you pop the bowl in the freezer.) On a floured board roll out some of the mixture very thinly, to 3 mm ($\frac{1}{8}$ in). Use a 6.5 cm ($2\frac{1}{2}$ in) plain cutter to cut out the rounds. Place a piece of walnut or a flaked almond in the centre of each biscuit. Use up all the mixture in this way. Bake on a greased tray in a moderate oven for 8–10 minutes. The biscuits become crisp as they cool on a wire rack.

To freeze: Pack in eights in a plastic bag. Then put the bags in a container — these biscuits are fairly fragile.
To use: Thaw at room temperature for 1 hour.

Cinnamon Cookies

I have an American friend whose kitchen seems always to be filled with the fragrant smell of hot cinnamon cookies. Here is her recipe. They are particularly nice served warm with a really good cup of coffee.

Cooking time: 10–15 minutes
Oven: 180°C, 350°F, Gas Mark 4
A baking tray, greased
Quantity: about 30 cookies

	METRIC	IMPERIAL
Soft margarine	170 g	6 oz
Light soft brown sugar	170 g	6 oz
1 egg		
Plain flour	285 g	10 oz
Ground cinnamon	2 × 5 ml spoons	2 teaspoons
Rolled oats	55 g	2 oz
Demerara sugar	55 g	2 oz
Ground cinnamon	½ × 5 ml spoon	½ teaspoon

Cream the margarine and sugar together until fluffy. Beat in the egg. Gradually mix in the flour and cinnamon until you have a soft dough. In a small bowl mix together the oats, demerara sugar and cinnamon. Take heaped teaspoonfuls of dough, form into a ball and roll in the oats mixture. As you put them on to the prepared tray slightly flatten them. Bake in a moderate oven for 10–15 minutes. Cool on a wire tray.

To freeze: Pack in tens in plastic bags.
To use: Thaw at room temperature for 1 hour.

Jumbles

This is a recipe from the fifteenth century, said to have been found on the battlefield of Bosworth, where it had been dropped by Richard III's cook. Anyway, they are delicious.

Cooking time: 12–15 minutes
Oven: 180°C, 350°F, Gas Mark 4
A baking sheet, greased
Quantity: about 40 biscuits

	METRIC	IMPERIAL
Plain flour	225 g	8 oz
Caster sugar	140 g	5 oz
Unsalted butter	140 g	5 oz
1 large egg		

Mix the flour and sugar together in a bowl. Cut the butter into pieces the size of a walnut. Rub in the butter until the mixture resembles breadcrumbs. Mix to a dough with the beaten egg. Take heaped teaspoonfuls of the mix and roll them in your hands to form a sausage. Roll each in caster sugar and place on a well-greased baking tray so that each is in the shape of the letter S. Bake in a moderate oven for 10–15 minutes, until golden. Remove from the tray with a flexible knife and allow to cool on a wire rack.

To freeze: Pack carefully in plastic bags and store in a container.
To use: Thaw in bags at room temperature for 1 hour.

Digestive Biscuits

These are immensely useful to have in reserve in the freezer or biscuit tin. They are marvellous with cheese for a quick lunch, or they can be half-dipped in melted chocolate for tea. Then children love them — especially if they have dipped them in themselves! Young children usually find it easier to decorate the biscuit with half a teaspoon of melted chocolate, by trailing it across and around the biscuit to make a pattern.

Cooking time: 15–20 minutes
Oven: 180°C, 350°F, Gas Mark 4
A baking tray, greased
Quantity: about 20 biscuits

	METRIC	IMPERIAL
Wholewheat flour	225 g	8 oz
Dark soft brown sugar	30 g	1 oz
Bicarbonate of soda	$\frac{1}{4} \times$ 5 ml spoon	$\frac{1}{4}$ teaspoon
Soft margarine	85 g	3 oz
1 egg yolk (or half of a whole egg)		
Milk	3×15 ml spoons	3 tablespoons

Mix all the dry ingredients together in a bowl. Cut the margarine into the mixture with a knife and then, if necessary, gently rub it in with the fingertips until absorbed. Stir the egg and milk together and mix into the flour with a knife until you have a soft dough. Knead this a little with your fingers. On a floured board, roll out the mixture thinly to 3 mm ($\frac{1}{8}$ in) thick. Cut out the biscuits with a 6.5 cm ($2\frac{1}{2}$ in) plain or fluted cutter. Bake on a greased baking tray just above the centre of a moderate oven for 15–20 minutes, until they are just becoming golden at the edges. Cool on a wire rack.

To freeze: Pack in tens in plastic bags.
To use: Thaw at room temperature for 1 hour.

Thimble Cookies

These were the first cookies I ever made. (At the age of three, and with a little help!) They were always firm favourites with us as children. They have a soft, cake-like consistency which makes them very popular. And they are, of course, easy to make.

Cooking time: 15–20 minutes
Oven: 180°C, 350°F, Gas Mark 4
2 baking sheets, greased, and a thimble
Quantity: 12 cookies

	METRIC	IMPERIAL
Soft margarine	85 g	3 oz
Vanilla flavoured caster sugar	85 g	3 oz
1 egg yolk		
Self-raising flour	170 g	6 oz
A pinch of salt		
Raspberry jam	2–3 × 15 ml spoons	2–3 tablespoons

Cream the margarine and sugar until pale and creamy. Beat in the egg yolk. Gradually add the flour and salt until all the dough is stiff. Knead into a ball. On a floured board, roll out some of the dough to 3 cm ($\frac{1}{8}$ in) thick. Using a 6.5 cm ($2\frac{1}{2}$ in) fluted cutter, cut out twelve circles. Place six of them on the baking sheet with room for expansion. Put a coffeespoon of red (or yellow) jam in the centre of each circle. Using a thimble, cut the centre from each of the other six circles and lower the tops on to the bases on the sheet. Brush with milk and sprinkle with a little granulated sugar. Repeat with the other baking sheet. Bake in the centre of a moderate oven for 15–20 minutes, until golden at the edges. Cool on tray for 5 minutes, then transfer to a wire rack.

To freeze: Pack in small plastic bags or a lidded container.
To use: Thaw at room temperature for 2 hours.

Brandy Snaps

If shortbread is the queen of biscuits, brandy snaps are the king. In my experience they are the least easy of all biscuits to make, but once you have found the right kind of baking tray you are as good as there. I will use only the pale grey, very smooth aluminium ones (mine say Prestige No 5714, $13\frac{1}{2} \times 9\frac{1}{2} \times \frac{5}{8}$ on the underside). These are also, incidentally, my favourite tins for swiss rolls. For brandy snaps I use the underside of the tin, well greased.

The other essential item for making brandy snaps is a supply either of wooden spoons with handles of 1 cm ($\frac{1}{2}$ in) diameter, or of lengths of wooden dowelling. I find that with up to sixteen lengths of dowelling, each about 15 cm (6 in) long, I can make brandy snaps in succession quite fast. It also helps to have heat-proof fingers!

Brandy snaps freeze exceptionally well, so I always make my Christmas ones at the beginning of December. A few always get broken; keep these separately (if you can stop yourself eating them) in a sealed container, for combining with your next orange mousse or for sprinkling on yoghourt. I usually serve brandy snaps with whipped cream. Pipe the cream into each end of the biscuit just before serving. They then become a real treat for tea, or for a pudding.

Cooking time: 8 minutes
Oven: 170°C, 325°F, Gas Mark 3
A baking tray, well-greased (and see note above)
You will also need a wide palette knife
Quantity: about 30

	METRIC	IMPERIAL
Butter or soft margarine	115 g	4 oz
Demerara sugar	115 g	4 oz
Golden syrup	115 g	4 oz
Plain flour	115 g	4 oz

171

A pinch of salt

Ground ginger	1 × 5 ml spoon	1 teaspoon
Lemon juice	1 × 5 ml spoon	1 teaspoon
Brandy	1 × 5 ml spoon	1 teaspoon

In a saucepan gently heat the butter, sugar and syrup until the butter has melted and the sugar is completely dissolved. Remove from heat and cool slightly. Sift (very important) the flour and salt and ginger into the mixture, stir well and add the lemon juice and brandy. Use a teaspoon to drop very well spaced blobs of mixture (only six to a tray) on to the greased baking tray. Bake in a very moderate oven for 8 minutes (I always use a timer for this). After removing from oven, leave for 30 seconds before very carefully lifting off the snaps with a palette knife. Have a wooden spoon handle (or piece of dowel) ready, and at once start wrapping the brandy snap around it, not too tightly. Leave on a wire rack to cool and proceed to the next snap. (If the last one or two on the tray have hardened, pop the tray back in the oven for a minute.) When the snaps have hardened on the handles (after about 3–4 minutes), gently remove the handles or pieces of dowel.

To freeze: Pack carefully in eights in plastic bags as soon as they have cooled, and store in a closed container.
To use: Thaw at room temperature for 1 hour.

Smilers

I always make these biscuits for children's parties. They use a shortcake biscuit mixture in vanilla and chocolate flavours. Once you've discovered how well the two mixtures combine during cooking, you will be able to make up your own cookie designs — for instance, animals with spots, or houses with chocolate doors and windows.

Cooking time: 12 minutes
Oven: 180°C, 350°F, Gas Mark 4
A baking tray, greased
Quantity: 16 biscuits

	METRIC	IMPERIAL
Vanilla shortcake mix:		
Soft margarine	115 g	4 oz
Caster sugar	55 g	2 oz
Plain flour	140 g	5 oz
A few drops of vanilla essence		
Chocolate shortcake mix:		
Soft margarine	115 g	4 oz
Caster sugar	55 g	2 oz
Plain flour	130 g	4½ oz
Cocoa	2 × 15 ml spoons	2 tablespoons
Drinking chocolate	2 × 15 ml spoons	2 tablespoons

For each flavour, cream the margarine and sugar until fluffy and then gradually work in the other ingredients until a soft dough is formed. Knead well with fingers. Roll out the vanilla mixture on a floured board to 6 mm (¼ in) thick. Use a 6 cm (2¼ in) round cutter to cut as many biscuits as you can. Place these on a greased baking tray. Now roll out the chocolate mixture in just the same way. Using a crescent-shaped cutter for a mouth, thimble-sized circles for eyes and a triangle for a nose, cut out these shapes (or any others you prefer) and gently position them on the vanilla rounds to make faces. The mouths can be made to curve up or down. (For the cake stall packs, I usually put in seven smilers to one 'misery', with instructions that the 'misery' should be eaten first!) Then repeat the biscuits with chocolate faces and vanilla features. Bake in a moderate oven for 12 minutes, until the vanilla part is pale gold. Leave for 1–2 minutes to cool, then remove with a knife and cool on a wire rack.

To freeze: Pack in eights in plastic bags.
To use: Thaw in bags at room temperature for 1 hour.

Whirligig Cookies

I make these for firework parties, since the cookies look rather like pin-wheels. But their attractive appearance makes them a popular tea-time item. These cookies use the same two mixes as in Smilers.

Cooking time: 12 minutes
Oven: 180°C, 350°F, Gas Mark 4
A baking tray, greased
Quantity: 16 biscuits

This time, roll out the chocolate mixture on one floured board to 6 mm (¼ in) thickness, then cut the sides with a knife to give the biggest rectangle. On another floured board, roll out the vanilla mixture and cut the same size rectangle. Lower the vanilla sheet on to the chocolate sheet and roll the two up together as in a swiss roll, starting with the longest side.

Wrap the roll in a polythene bag or put a cloth over it, and store the roll and the board in the fridge for 1 hour or in the freezer for ½ hour. The dough is easier to work when it is really cold. Then cut off slices from the roll 6 mm (¼ in) thick, and bake them on the prepared tray for 12 minutes. Cool for 1 minute, then remove and allow to finish cooling on a wire rack.

To freeze: Pack in eights in plastic bags.
To use: Thaw in bags at room temperature for 1 hour.

Chequerboard Cookies

I find these are firm favourites with adults as well as with children. Make up the vanilla dough and chocolate dough as given in the recipe for Smilers.

Cooking time: 12 minutes
Oven: 180°C, 350°F, Gas Mark 4
A baking tray, greased
Quantity: 16 biscuits

Knock each dough into the shape of a brick, so that each side can be cut into three strips to give nine very long chip-like pieces. Now make up new brick-shaped pieces of dough by exchanging every other strip for the alternate flavour, so that at each end of the brick you have a chess-board effect. Gently press the dough from each side to make the pieces stick to each other.

Rest the bricks in the fridge for ½ hour to prevent distortion when slicing. Then cut 6 mm (¼ in) thick slices from the bricks and bake on greased trays for 12 minutes. Leave to cool on wire racks.

To freeze: Pack in eights in plastic bags.
To use: Thaw at room temperature for 1 hour.

MHA (Must Have Another) Snaps

This is a drop cookie with a particularly more-ish flavour. I devised these after local bee society meetings, where we always have honey in our coffee. They are very quick and easy to make. Get your friends to guess what is in them!

Cooking time: 10–15 minutes
Oven: 190°C, 375°F, Gas Mark 5
A baking tray, greased
Quantity: about 24 biscuits

	METRIC	IMPERIAL
Soft margarine	115 g	4 oz
Light soft brown sugar	55 g	2 oz

Clear honey	1 × 15 ml spoon	1 tablespoon
A few drops of vanilla essence		
Instant coffee powder	1 × 15 ml spoon	1 tablespoon
Plain flour	115 g	4 oz

Cream the margarine, sugar, honey, vanilla and coffee together until fluffy and creamy. Mix in the flour until all is combined. Then drop the mixture in teaspoonfuls on to the prepared tray, and bake in a moderately hot oven for 10–15 minutes. Leave to cool on a wire rack.

To freeze: Pack into small bags.
To use: Thaw in bags at room temperature for 1 hour.

Gingerbread Men

No child should have reached the age of five without making these splendid biscuits — a wholly educational experience. I find children like to use currants or chocolate drops to make eyes, mouth and buttons. When I make them for presents (often to accompany the Ladybird story book), or for tying on the Christmas tree, I decorate them with piped icing, giving the girls and the boys rather elaborate Bavarian clothes. For the cake stall I pack one Hansel and Gretel together, and they look very pretty tied up with a decorative ribbon.

Cooking time: 15 minutes
Oven: 200°C, 400°F, Gas Mark 6
A baking tray, greased
Quantity: about 12 biscuits
You will need a Gingerbread Man cutter. I use a very good Tala one in the shape of a woman, and cut a V section out of the skirt to turn it into a man

	METRIC	IMPERIAL
Self-raising flour	225 g	8 oz
Dark soft brown sugar	85 g	3 oz
Salt	1 × 5 ml spoon	1 teaspoon
Ground ginger	2 × 5 ml spoons	2 teaspoons
Mixed spice	1 × 5 ml spoon	1 teaspoon
Soft margarine	115 g	4 oz
Milk	3 × 15 ml spoons	3 tablespoons

A few currants or chocolate drops

Sieve all the dry ingredients together in a bowl. Cut the margarine into the bowl, and rub it in until the mixture resembles breadcrumbs. Mix to a dough with the milk. On a floured board roll out to 6 mm ($\frac{1}{4}$ in) thickness. Cut out as many biscuits as possible. Place them on the greased baking tray, and decorate with currants. Use the rest of the mixture to make more. Bake in a hot oven for 15 minutes. Leave on tray for 2 minutes before transferring to a wire tray.

To freeze: Freeze in a box on top of each other.
To use: Thaw at room temperature for 1 hour. You can ice them before freezing, or after they have thawed.

Christmas Cookies

I use these Christmas cookies as Christmas tree decorations or as stocking fillers. They look very pretty as a table decoration, or on a cake stall tied to some branches made into a little tree. I make my own shapes from cardboard — a bell, a Christmas tree and a star. They look appealing when iced in red and white with silver, gold and green ball dragées. Don't forget the hole for a ribbon tie.

Cooking time: 10–12 minutes
Oven: 180°C, 350°F, Gas Mark 4
A baking tray, greased
Quantity: about 20 cookies

	METRIC	IMPERIAL
Soft margarine	115 g	4 oz
Caster sugar	115 g	4 oz
Golden syrup	4 × 15 ml spoons	4 tablespoons
Plain flour	255 g	9 oz
Bicarbonate of soda	$\frac{1}{2}$ × 5 ml spoon	$\frac{1}{2}$ teaspoon
Ground ginger	1 × 5 ml spoon	1 teaspoon
Icing:		
Icing sugar	115 g	4 oz
Hot water		

Cream the margarine and sugar until fluffy. Add the syrup and beat well. Gradually mix in the sieved flour, bicarbonate and ginger until you have a soft dough. On a floured board roll some dough out to 6 mm ($\frac{1}{4}$ in) thickness, and use a cutter to cut out biscuits or cut round your own shapes with the end of a pointed knife. With a wooden cocktail stick or metal skewer, make a hole near the top but not too near the edge. Don't make the hole too small — it will shrink in baking. Bake the biscuits in a moderate oven on a greased tray for 10–12 minutes, until golden. Cool on a wire rack. Make the icing by mixing the sieved icing sugar with a little hot water. Then ice all over and decorate with silver balls. Or you can pipe stiffer icing around the edge of each shape and put balls at intervals along the line. Use paper wrapping ribbon to make the loops.

To freeze: Store iced or plain in boxes.
To use: Thaw in container at room temperature for 1 hour.

Almond Currant Rings

I make these all the year round. But at Christmas I decorate them as holly wreaths, with icing and red ball dragées or pieces of glacé cherry and a ribbon.

Cooking time: 10–12 minutes
Oven: 200°C. 400°F. Gas Mark 6
A baking tray, greased
Quantity: about 24

	METRIC	IMPERIAL
Plain flour	225 g	8 oz
Ground rice	55 g	2 oz
Caster sugar	140 g	5 oz
Soft margarine	170 g	6 oz
Currants	115 g	4 oz
1 egg (or 2 yolks, with 15 ml —		
1 tablespoon — of milk)		
Almond essence	$\frac{1}{2}$ × 5 ml spoon	$\frac{1}{2}$ teaspoon

Rub the margarine into the flour, ground rice and sugar mixture. Stir in the currants, and mix in the egg and almond essence. Knead together to form a dough. On a floured board roll out to 6 mm ($\frac{1}{4}$ in) thick, and cut rounds with a 7.5 mm (3 in) fluted cutter. Then remove the centres with a 2.5 cm (1 in) fluted cutter. Gently move the rings on to a greased baking tray. Bake in a hot oven for 10–12 minutes until just changing colour. Remove from tray and leave to cool on a wire rack.

To freeze: Pack in eights in bags, or make an assortment of Christmas biscuits and pack together.
To use: Thaw at room temperature for 1 hour in container.

Lemon Raisin Refrigerator Cookies

If you are busy (and who isn't?), always keep a plastic bag with some cookie dough in the fridge. It will keep quite happily for a week. This is a useful recipe with storage in mind because it helps the full flavour of the lemon (or orange) to develop.

Cooking time: 15 minutes
Oven: 180°C, 350°F, Gas Mark 4
A baking tray, greased
Quantity: about 36

	METRIC	IMPERIAL
Soft margarine	170 g	6 oz
Soft light brown sugar	85 g	3 oz
Caster sugar	85 g	3 oz
The grated rind of a lemon (or orange)		
1 large egg		
Plain flour	290 g	10 oz
Baking powder	1 × 5 ml spoon	1 teaspoon
Raisins or nuts	55 g	2 oz

Cream the margarine, sugars and lemon (or orange) rind until fluffy. Add the beaten egg, and mix in the flour, baking powder and raisins. Mix well to form a soft dough. Make two rolls with the dough, about 5 cm (2 in) across. Store in plastic bags in the fridge for 2 hours, overnight or a week. When required, slice off thin slices with a hot knife (dipped in water and dried), using a gentle sawing action. Bake on greased trays in a moderate oven for 15 minutes. Remove to cool on a wire tray.

To freeze: Pack in bags and store in containers.
To use: Thaw at room temperature for 1 hour.

GERALDENE HOLT'S CAKE STALL

SPECIAL CAKES

These are the cakes that are so enjoyable to make for all sorts of special occasions, whenever there is an excuse for celebrating — birthdays, anniversaries, Christmas, Easter, November 5th. But I also like to make a special cake at the end of the school term, to celebrate a new job, when school exams are over, the arrival of visitors, or to give as a present. I feel that as a country we just don't celebrate often enough: celebrating makes everyone happier. And it's such a nice idea to name a cake specially for the occasion or person.

My first cake is named after my daughter, who chose this scrumptious meringue cake with chocolate cream as her birthday cake for three years running!

Gâteau Madeleine

This is made up of three layers of crisp meringue Suisse, sandwiched with chocolate chantilly cream and decorated with chocolate shavings, known as chocolate caraque. The meringue rounds can be made at any time and kept in a sealed container for 3–4 weeks.

Cooking time: 2 hours, plus overnight to cool
Oven: 100°C, 200°F, Gas Mark ¼
3 baking sheets, covered with 'Bakewell' silicone paper

	METRIC	IMPERIAL
4 egg whites		
Caster sugar	225 g	8 oz
Chocolate cream:		
Plain chocolate	225 g	8 oz
Water	4 × 15 ml spoons	4 tablespoons
Double cream	570 g	1 pint
Chocolate caraque:		
Plain chocolate	55 g	2 oz

Draw three 20 cm (8 in) circles around plates on to the 'Bakewell' vegetable parchment paper. Put a smear of margarine at the corner of each baking sheet to hold the paper in place, smoothing it flat as you do so.

Now whisk the egg whites until really stiff. Fold in half the sugar and then whisk again before folding in the rest of the sugar. Spread or pipe the mixture into three rounds, keeping the edge just within the drawn circle. Make the meringue circles as level as possible. Bake in the cool oven for 50–60 minutes and then change round their positions in the oven. Bake for 1 hour more. Then turn off the oven and allow to cool overnight. Next day peel the paper from the meringues and store them in a lidded container.

To make the chocolate cream, very gently melt the broken chocolate with the water in a small bowl over hot water. Remove from heat and allow to cool a little. Whip the cream in a large bowl until it thickens but still looks glossy. Now carefully pour in the melted chocolate and whip all together until thick. Sandwich the meringue rounds with the cream and spread it over the top and sides too.

To make the caraque, melt the 55 g (2 oz) of chocolate on a plate over hot water. Pour on to a marble slab or laminate surface. Leave to set. When the chocolate is set, take a long, sharp knife and scrape very thin curling layers. Hold the knife nearly upright and, using a sawing movement, drag the knife towards you (away from you is safer) and so form a scroll of thin chocolate. Gently lift the scroll and place on top of the cake. Repeat until you have covered the top of the cake and used up the chocolate. Then put the whole gâteau in the refrigerator for 2–3 hours before serving, or in the freezer if you are storing it overnight.

To freeze: For longer than overnight, I cut the gâteau into portions and then freeze in lidded boxes.
To use: This gâteau thaws very quickly. It is particularly good if eaten, like ice cream, when half frozen.

Christmas Cake

I have made this cake hundred' of times and it's always good. It is dark and moist and fruity, keeps extremely well and actually improves if kept for about 4 weeks. I also use it as a celebration cake for birthdays, anniversaries and weddings. People tell me they are often worried about leaving an ingredient out of their Christmas cake. There are two ways of dealing with this problem: either mark your recipe as you add each ingredient or, better still, collect every ingredient together on plates and saucers or pieces of paper and check them against the recipe before you begin. Check also that every plate is empty before you put the mixture in the cake tin!

For a Christmas or anniversary cake I prefer a square tin (20 cm (8 in)). I think it cuts much more economically (up to fifty people) and it's easier and more effective to decorate. I usually marzipan my Christmas cake 1 week before Christmas, and ice and decorate it 4 days before. I always leave the icing with a roughened snow scene effect; I highlight this with a red satin ribbon laid diagonally across the cake but just off centre (cut the ends in neat V-shapes). The addition of a five-looped bow fastened with a pin two-thirds of the way along the ribbon strip, and a piece of pretty holly, is all that is needed to give a very effective festive touch.

Cooking time: $3\frac{1}{2}$–4 hours
Oven: 150°C, 300°F, Gas Mark 2 for $1\frac{1}{2}$ hours; 140°C, 275°F, Gas Mark 1 for 2–$2\frac{1}{2}$ hours
A 20 cm (8 in) square tin or a 23 cm (9 in) round one, greased and well-lined on base and sides

	METRIC	IMPERIAL
Butter	225 g	8 oz
Dark soft brown sugar	225 g	8 oz
Black treacle	2 × 15 ml spoons	2 tablespoons
4 large eggs		
Plain flour	290 g	10 oz
Bicarbonate of soda	$\frac{1}{4}$ × 5 ml spoon	$\frac{1}{4}$ teaspoon
Salt	$\frac{1}{2}$ × 5 ml spoon	$\frac{1}{2}$ teaspoon
Mixed spice	1 × 5 ml spoon	1 teaspoon
Cinnamon	$\frac{1}{2}$ × 5 ml spoon	$\frac{1}{2}$ teaspoon
Ground allspice or nutmeg	$\frac{1}{2}$ × 5 ml spoon	$\frac{1}{2}$ teaspoon
Seedless raisins	225 g	8 oz
Chopped seeded raisins (optional)	55 g	2 oz
Sultanas	225 g	8 oz

Currants	225 g	8 oz
Glacé cherries, quartered	115 g	4 oz
Chopped candied peel	115 g	4 oz
Chopped blanched almonds	55 g	2 oz
Sherry, stout or milk	2 × 15 ml spoons	2 tablespoons

Cream the butter and sugar until fluffy and much lighter in colour. Gradually beat in the treacle and eggs, adding a little of the flour towards the end. Sieve the remaining flour, bicarbonate of soda, salt and spices on to the egg mixture and give a few stirs. Now add the fruit and nuts to the bowl, along with the liquid. Stir well with a wooden spoon until all the ingredients are combined. I usually have a quick taste at this stage — cook's perks! Now spoon or pour the mixture into the prepared tin, smoothing it level. Bake first just below the centre of a slow oven for 1½ hours. Then lower the oven temperature to 150°C (275°F, Gas Mark 1) and bake for a further 2–2½ hours. Allow the cake to cool in its tin before turning out and removing the baking papers. Wrap it in fresh greaseproof paper and store in a lidded container. After a week you can, if you wish, unwrap the cake, pierce holes with a skewer and pour brandy, rum or sherry into the cake. Then re-wrap and store again. It depends whether you prefer to eat or drink your alcohol!

Marzipan

This is a delicious sweetmeat in its own right (I find it quite difficult to stop myself eating it). Marzipan is tremendously useful in baking, all the year round — and not just as an almond paste underneath icing. I use it in Danish pastries, to make petalled flowers, etc, for cake decorations, as a filling in pies underneath fruit, for stuffing dates, to make sweets, and as an icing in itself, in Battenberg cake or Simnel cake. For small fancy cakes, you can cut a large sponge cake into shapes and cover their tops and sides with marzipan before icing. Marzipan is very satisfying to make at home — a kind of edible clay. But sometimes it pays to buy good quality commercially-made marzipan on a pre-Christmas offer.

Marzipan to cover top and sides of a 20—23 cm (8—9 in) cake:

	METRIC	IMPERIAL
Icing sugar	170 g	6 oz
Caster sugar	170 g	6 oz
Ground almonds	340 g	12 oz
1 egg		
Lemon juice	2 × 5 ml spoons	2 teaspoons
Brandy	2 × 5 ml spoons	2 teaspoons
Almond essence	¼ × 5 ml spoon	¼ teaspoon

Sieve the icing sugar into a bowl. Stir in the caster sugar and the ground almonds. In a cup mix the egg, lemon juice, brandy and almond essence. Pour on to the mixture in the bowl and stir well together until a smooth, firm dough is formed. The marzipan can be wrapped in greaseproof paper and kept in a plastic bag in the fridge for some weeks.

To marzipan the Christmas cake, dust a board with icing sugar and roll out on to it half the marzipan, shaped to fit the top of the cake. Brush the top of the cake with sieved apricot jam, or apple jelly (I usually use this, to save sieving). Lower the cake on to the marzipan, upside down, and use a sharp knife held upright to cut off any surplus marzipan. Now knead the marzipan scraps in with the other half and divide in two. Roll out in two long narrow strips to fit the sides of the cake. (I cut against a ruler, to get a straight edge.) Brush jam on to the sides of the cake and roll the cake on to the marzipan strips. Make sure your joins are not at the corners of the cake. Stand the cake the right way up, and roll it all over with a rolling-pin, making sure you have smoothed over the joins well. Leave it loosely wrapped in a tea cloth for 2–3 days so that it can dry out before you ice it.

ROYAL ICING

If marzipanning the cake is fun, icing it is pure enjoyment. If you can use an electric beater to make the royal icing, so much the better; otherwise, wait until you feel energetic and use a good-sized bowl and a wooden spoon. It will take 5–10 minutes hard beating but you will be pleased with the result.

Royal icing can be very hard and almost impossible to eat unless an emulsifier is added in the form of glycerine or honey. So my recipe includes this. But if you really prefer a rock-like icing, leave it out.

Royal icing for the top and sides of a 20–23 cm (8–9 in) cake:

	METRIC	IMPERIAL
Icing sugar	900 g	2 lb
4 egg whites (at room temp.)		
Lemon juice	2 × 5 ml spoons	2 teaspoons
Glycerine	2 × 5 ml spoons	2 teaspoons

Sieve the icing sugar into a bowl, then store it on a plate or piece of paper. Beat the egg whites in a good-sized bowl until frothy. Gradually add half the icing sugar in spoonfuls, beating it in well each time. Now beat well for 5–10 minutes until the icing grows in bulk and becomes quite fluffy. Add the lemon juice, glycerine and the other half of the icing sugar gradually, beating in well each time until the icing will stand up in peaks and has lost its shininess. Cover the bowl with a damp cloth if you are not using the icing straight away.

188

To ice the marzipanned cake, use a broad-bladed knife or spatula and spread the icing generously over the sides and top of the cake until there is an even thickness of icing. Now use the end of a smaller knife to swirl the icing and make a roughened snow effect, making sure that you haven't lost the shape of the cake. Now cut a piece of red ribbon almost as long as the diagonal or diameter of the cake, cut a V-shape out of each end to improve the effect and gently lay the ribbon on the wet icing. Use a ruler to smooth the ribbon flat if necessary. Use more ribbon to make a looped bow (don't tie it) with five or six loops, and pin them together. In the centre of the bow pin a sprig of holly, or two artificial poinsettia flowers and leaves, and then pin the whole arrangement to the flat ribbon about two-thirds of the way along the cake. Store unwrapped for 3 days to allow the icing to dry out.

Coffee Cream Gâteau

This celebration cake is popular at any time of the year. It's very good for a dinner party, since the cake can be assembled in the morning and left in the fridge until the evening. Thin layers of coffee sponge are sandwiched with French butter cream, and decorated with toasted almonds and flaked coffee-flavoured chocolate.

Cooking time: 45–50 minutes
Oven: 190°C, 375°F, Gas Mark 5
2 × 20 cm (8 in) sandwich tins, at least 4 cm ($1\frac{1}{2}$ in) deep, greased and base-lined with greased paper

	METRIC	IMPERIAL
Butter	225 g	8 oz
Caster sugar	225 g	8 oz
4 eggs		
Coffee essence	1 × 15 ml spoon	1 tablespoon

189

Self-raising flour	225 g	8 oz
Coffee cream:		
Caster sugar	225 g	8 oz
Water	2 × 15 ml spoons	2 tablespoons
4 egg yolks, whisked		
Unsalted butter	225 g	8 oz
Coffee essence	4–6 × 5 ml spoons	4–6 teaspoons
Blanched almonds	55 g	2 oz
Coffee-flavoured chocolate	55 g	2 oz

Cream the butter and sugar until really light and fluffy. Beat in the coffee essence and eggs, adding them gradually. Carefully fold in the sifted flour. Spoon the mixture into the two prepared tins: put each filled tin on the scales to check that you've divided the mixture equally. Bake in the middle of a moderately hot oven for 45–50 minutes until the cakes are golden brown and spring back when pressed. Leave in tins for 3 minutes before turning out to cool on wire racks.

To make the coffee cream, heat the caster sugar and water very gently in a fairly heavy saucepan until the sugar is completely dissolved. Then bring to the boil, and let it boil for 5 minutes until it reaches 105°C (220°F), if you have a sugar thermometer: otherwise, until the syrup forms a thread when pulled between thumb and finger. (Cool a little syrup in a teaspoon before you try.)

Pour quickly in a steady stream on to the whisked egg yolks. Continue whisking, and add the butter a small lump at a time until all of it has been incorporated. Whisk the cream until it is smooth and fluffy, and gradually whisk in the coffee essence. Now carefully slice each cake in half with a long serrated knife and a gentle sawing action. Sandwich each layer with coffee cream, then use the rest — except for 4 tablespoons — to cover the sides and top of the gâteau.

Flake the blanched almonds, put them on a heatproof plate or tin, and toast them under the grill for 2–3 minutes until they are golden. Don't take your eyes off the almonds — it happens quite quickly! Immediately remove them from the heat and allow the almonds to cool. Then gently press the toasted almonds into the sides of the gâteau. Decorate the top of the gâteau with the coffee cream you have kept in reserve. Pipe or spoon a pattern of 10–12 whirls around the rim of the cake. Cover the top of the cake with grated or chopped coffee-flavoured chocolate. Let it develop full flavour by keeping it cold for several hours.

To freeze: This gâteau can be frozen if you are too busy to eat it. Store it in a lidded container. Place the gâteau on the inverted lid and lower the base of the container on to it. Make sure you label it to show which way up it is to be stored.
To use: Allow to thaw in its container very slowly at room temperature overnight.

Simnel Cake

Simnel cake is a lovely, delicately flavoured fruit cake traditionally baked by a daughter to give to her mother on Mothering Sunday. I like to keep this tradition going. My mother then often keeps her Simnel cake for Easter.

Cooking time: 2¾–3 hours
Oven: 170°C, 300°F, Gas Mark 2
An 18 cm (7 in) round tin, greased and the base and sides lined with greased paper

	METRIC	IMPERIAL
Butter or soft margarine	170 g	6 oz
Soft light brown sugar	170 g	6 oz
3 eggs		
Finely grated rind of		
1 orange or 1 lemon		

Plain flour	225 g	8 oz
Baking powder	1 × 5 ml spoon	1 teaspoon
A pinch of salt		
Mixed spice	1 × 5 ml spoon	1 teaspoon
Sultanas	225 g	8 oz
Currants	170 g	6 oz
Raisins	55 g	2 oz
Glacé cherries (quartered)	55 g	2 oz
Chopped candied peel	55 g	2 oz
Milk	2 × 15 ml spoons	2 tablespoons
Marzipan:		
Icing sugar	115 g	4 oz
Caster sugar	115 g	4 oz
Ground almonds	225 g	8 oz
1 egg yolk		
Lemon juice	2 × 5 ml spoons	2 teaspoons
2–3 drops of almond essence		
Icing:		
Icing sugar	55 g	2 oz
About 12 sugar flowers		

First of all make the marzipan: sieve the icing sugar into a bowl, and stir in the caster sugar and ground almonds. Mix to a soft dough with the egg yolk, lemon juice and almond essence. Knead until smooth and store in a plastic bag.

Now cream the butter and sugar until light and fluffy, and gradually beat in the egg and the grated lemon or orange rind. Sieve the flour, baking powder, salt and spice on to a plate and add to the mixture a little at a time, alternating with additions of the dried fruit. Combine all together with the milk.

Take the marzipan and divide it into two halves. Roll out one half to an 18 cm (7 in) circle (cut round the base of the tin, if necessary). Now spoon half the cake mixture into the tin and spread it level. Gently lower the circle of marzipan on to the mixture, using your fingertips to ensure it is level. Now spoon the rest of the cake mixture into the tin on top of the marzipan, and level it off with the back of a spoon. Bake in the centre of a slow oven for $2\frac{3}{4}$–3 hours, when the centre of the cake should be firm. Allow the cake to cool in its tin for 45 minutes before turning out to cool on a wire rack.

When the cake is cool, roll out the rest of the marzipan to an 18 cm (7 in) circle, and brush the top of the cake with apple jelly or sieved apricot jam. Fit the marzipan on top of the cake and press gently down. Use the prongs of a fork to press gently all around the edge to make a 1 cm ($\frac{1}{2}$ in) border. Brush the marzipan with a little beaten egg and gently toast under the grill until golden.

I usually then make a little glacé icing, made by mixing the icing sugar with 2 teaspoons of hot water, and pour this over the marzipan until the icing just reaches the forked border. Then arrange the sugar flowers in a pretty design on the icing or around its edge. Tie a ribbon around the side of the cake.

(The traditional decoration for a Simnel cake is twelve marzipan balls, set around the edge of the cake to represent the twelve apostles. If you choose to do this, remember to keep back some of the marzipan.)

Easter Nest Cake

I find that all children like a nest cake at Easter. Sometimes I make one as an Easter surprise, and on other occasions they enjoy helping to make it. I usually use a variation of the Marble cake recipe (see Tea-time and Family Cakes) as a basis but you could use any popular cake, like chocolate sponge or banana cake. If I use a Marble cake, I like to keep to the Easter colours of yellow, white and chocolate.

193

Here's how you make the icing and nest for an 18–20 cm (7–8 in) cake:

	METRIC	IMPERIAL
Icing sugar	225 g	8 oz
Soft margarine or butter	85 g	3 oz
Top of milk	4 × 15 ml spoons	4 tablespoons
2–3 drops of yellow colouring		
1–2 drops of lemon or banana flavouring		
Plain coating chocolate	115 g	4 oz
All-Bran or Shredded Wheat	55 g	2 oz
Corn Flakes or Bran Flakes	55 g	2 oz
10–12 miniature sugar-coated eggs		
10–12 assorted foil-wrapped chocolate eggs		
1 fluffy artificial chick		

Sieve the icing sugar into a bowl, blend in the soft margarine with a fork and mix to a smooth, spreading icing with the milk. Colour and flavour the icing as you wish — a pale lemon colour and flavour works well, or if chocolate is popular, add 1 × 15 ml spoon (1 tablespoon) cocoa mixed with 1 × 15 ml spoon (1 tablespoon) of hot water. Spread the icing over the top and sides of the cake. Allow it to set a little. Now melt the chocolate in a medium-sized bowl over a little hot water in a saucepan. When completely melted, stir in the breakfast cereals. If you haven't both kinds of cereal, just use double the amount of what you've got. Stir the chocolate mixture until all the cereal is well coated. Spoon half the mixture on to the top of the cake and smooth it into a circle covering at least two-thirds of the cake. Use the rest of the chocolate mixture to build up the wall of the nest, until you have a convincing nest-like structure that is not too deep. Leave to set, then fill with the miniature Easter eggs and one or two artificial chicks. Children like to make these with cotton wool.

Gâteau à l'Orange

This creamy gâteau has layers of featherlight sponge cake, separated by delicious orange filling and covered in an orange-flavoured cream.

Cooking time: 25 minutes
Oven: 190°C, 375°F, Gas Mark 5
2 19–20 cm (7½–8 in) sandwich tins, greased

	METRIC	IMPERIAL
4 standard eggs		
Caster sugar	115 g	4 oz
Plain flour	115 g	4 oz
Butter or soft margarine	30 g	1 oz
Orange filling and decoration:		
Water	150 ml	¼ pint
Custard powder	30 g	1 oz
Chopped orange marmalade	4 round 15 ml spoons	4 round tablespoons
Butter	15 g	½ oz
Mandarin oranges or orange slices	1 can (312 g)	1 can (11 oz)
Toasted desiccated coconut	15 g	½ oz
Double cream	150 ml	¼ pint
Cointreau	2 × 15 ml spoons	2 tablespoons

Sieve the flour into a bowl (twice if you have time). In a warmed bowl place the warmed sugar and the eggs. Whisk the mixture until it is really pale, thick and foamy, so that a trail is left across the top of the mixture. Very gently sieve some of the flour on to the mixture and carefully fold it in with a metal spoon. If using an electric whisk, detach the whisk and fold in the flour with it. Continue to fold in the flour *very gently*, alternately with the butter which you must first warm in a cup or small saucepan until it is all melted. When both flour and butter are incorporated, pour the mixture into the prepared tins and bake in the centre of a moderately hot oven for 25 minutes, until golden, well risen and springy to the touch. Leave them to rest for 1 minute in the tins before turning on to a wire rack to cool.

To make the orange filling and decoration, toast the coconut on a plate under the grill for 2–3 minutes, watching all the time until it turns golden. Leave to cool on the plate. Now make the orange filling by blending 1 tablespoon of the water with the custard powder in a cup. Heat the rest of the water with the marmalade in a small saucepan. Bring to boil, pour on to the custard mixture, return to saucepan and cook until thick and clear (about 2–3 minutes), stirring all the time. Remove from heat, beat in the butter and leave to cool.

With a long, finely serrated knife carefully split each cake into two layers. Spread each layer with some of the orange filling and assemble into a gâteau, spreading more filling over its sides too. Coat the sides with the toasted coconut by rolling the cake in the plate. Brush the top of the cake evenly with the remaining marmalade mixture. Drain the mandarin or orange segments and arrange them on top of the cake, leaving the rim free. Now whip the double cream until thick, whip in the cointreau and pipe the cream around the rim of the gâteau and at the base of the sides. Keep it cool in a fridge for at least 2 hours, to allow the flavours to mellow.

Devil's Food Cake

This is the most famous of American cakes. It is very delicious and uses American frosting, which is made from egg whites and caster sugar. It's a very useful kind of icing to know how to make — try coffee- and orange-flavoured versions too.

Cooking time: 35–40 minutes
Oven: 170°C, 325°F, Gas Mark 3
3 × 18 cm (7 in) sandwich tins (if you only have 2 tins, use one twice), or 2 × 20 cm (8 in) tins, greased and base-lined

196

	METRIC	IMPERIAL
Self-raising flour	170 g	6 oz
Baking powder	2 × 5 ml spoons	2 teaspoons
Caster sugar	170 g	6 oz
Soft margarine	170 g	6 oz
4 eggs		
Cocoa	55 g	2 oz
Very hot water	6 × 15 ml spoons	6 tablespoons
Chocolate fudge filling:		
Icing sugar	170 g	6 oz
Soft margarine	55 g	2 oz
Plain chocolate	30 g	1 oz
American frosting:		
Caster sugar	340 g	12 oz
2 egg whites		
Hot water	4 × 15 ml spoons	4 tablespoons
Cream of tartar	¼ × 5 ml spoon	¼ teaspoon

Warm a fairly large bowl and tip in the sieved flour and baking powder, the sugar, soft margarine and the eggs. In a cup mix the cocoa with the very hot water and scrape this into the bowl. Mix all the ingredients together carefully with a wooden spoon, and then beat for 1–2 minutes. Divide the mixture between the two 20 cm (8 in) or the three 18 cm (7 in) tins. Bake in the centre of a moderate oven for 35–40 minutes. Leave in tins for 4 minutes before turning out to cool on a wire rack.

When the cakes are cool make the chocolate fudge filling. Sieve the icing sugar into a bowl and mix to a smooth, spreading icing with the soft margarine and melted chocolate. Sandwich the cakes with the filling.

Now put a large bowl over a saucepan of simmering water, and whisk in it (with a hand or electric beater) the sugar, egg whites, water and cream of tartar. The beating will take just about 7 minutes. Remove from the heat and beat until the frosting stands in soft peaks. Then spread it all over the Devil's Food cake, leaving a swirled design. Leave to set before serving the same day.

To freeze: Store the cake layers, with greaseproof paper between them, in a lidded plastic container.
To use: Thaw at room temperature for 3 hours, then make frosting and complete the cake.

Festive Ring

This is another American cake which I always make at Christmas, but it is nice at any time of the year. The fact that it will cut into sixteen slices makes it very useful for a party. It is also a good cake to give to a cake stall because it looks so pretty.

Cooking time: 45 minutes
Oven: 190°C, 375°F, Gas Mark 5
An 18–20 cm (7–8 in) ring cake tin 7–8 cm (2½–3 in) deep, well-greased

	METRIC	IMPERIAL
Soft margarine	170 g	6 oz
Caster sugar	170 g	6 oz
3 eggs		
Vanilla essence	½ × 5 ml spoon	½ teaspoon
Self-raising flour	170 g	6 oz
Icing and decoration:		
Icing sugar	170 g	6 oz
Hot water	3 × 5 ml spoons	3 teaspoons
4 glacé cherries		
Angelica	7 g	¼ oz
8 walnut halves or toasted almonds		

198

In a warmed bowl. cream the soft margarine and sugar until really light and fluffy. Gradually beat in the eggs and the vanilla essence. Fold in the sieved flour very gently. and then spoon the mixture into the ring tin. Smooth the top level all the way round. Bake in the centre of a moderately hot oven for 45 minutes. Leave in tin for 4 minutes to cool. before turning out on to a wire rack.

Make the icing by mixing the sieved icing sugar with the hot water until the icing is of pouring consistency. Using a dessert-spoon. spoon the icing over the cake so that the top is well covered all over. and the icing trails down the side to resemble a snow-capped mountain. Now cut the glacé cherries in half. wash and dry them if they are very sticky. and place them evenly round the cake. Place a nut in between each half cherry. With a sharp knife. cut diagonally across the strip of angelica and then cut again to make diamond-shaped leaves. Put one or two on either side of each cherry. Store in a lidded container.

To freeze: The entire cake with icing can be frozen. but I prefer to freeze just the cake in a lidded container and ice it when needed.
To use: Thaw at room temperature in container for 2 hours. then ice and decorate.

Roundabout Cake

This children's party cake is always a tremendous attraction. It is very easy to make. and has the added bonus of providing a small present for each child to keep. It is also a good cake if you are giving a party with a fairground theme.

Use as a basis one 20 cm (8 in) single-layer cake — chocolate is a good flavour. such as Favourite Chocolate Sponge (page 42) or Multicoloured Marble Cake (page 60).

	METRIC	IMPERIAL
Icing:		
Icing sugar	225 g	8 oz
Soft margarine	85 g	3 oz
Top of milk	3 × 15 ml spoons	3 tablespoons

A few drops of vanilla essence
Decoration:
One paper plate, decorated or plain
One cardboard tube (from inside a kitchen roll) or a knitting needle 30 cm (12 in) long
Decorative wrapping paper (optional)
At least 6 striped straws
100 g (¼ lb) dolly mixtures or Smarties
A number of animal rubbers — as many as there are children at the party

Make the icing by mixing together the sieved icing sugar, the soft margarine, the top of milk and the vanilla essence until smooth and spreadable. Cover the top and sides of the cake and put it on a flat serving platter.

Now make a straight cut in the paper plate from the rim to its centre (that is, along a radius) and overlap the cuts to give it a dished appearance (like a very flat cone). Secure the join with either glue, or sellotape (on the inside surface), or staples. If the plate is plain, now decorate it with stuck-on patterns or a crayon design, or stick on the dolly mixture sweets with egg white or sugar syrup. Decorate the cardboard tube with a strip of coloured paper to resemble a barber's pole, or simply cover it with wrapping paper or a crayon design. Fix the tube at one end to the inside centre of the plate with sticky tape, so that the tube is at right angles to the plate. Now firmly embed the tube in the middle of the cake (or, instead of the tube, use a knitting needle pushed through the centre of the plate and into the cake). Support the edge of the plate with straws, cut to length and embed in the icing at equal distances around the edge of the cake. Now decorate the sides of the cake with dolly mixture sweets arranged in a pretty design. Finally, place the animal rubbers (or you can use chocolate animals, like elephants and ducks) around the edge of the cake to resemble roundabout horses. To crown it all, write the child's name on a small flag, stick it to a cocktail stick and place it on the top of the roundabout.

Guy Fawkes Cake

If you are having a bonfire party on November 5th, a bonfire cake is great fun. My children very much enjoy making the Guy from marzipan — but you could use a Guy made from pipe cleaners and clothed in paper.

Cooking time: $1\frac{1}{4}$–$1\frac{1}{2}$ hours
Oven: 180°C, 350°F, Gas Mark 4
A 1 litre (2 pint) pudding basin (preferably a heatproof glass one with a rounded bottom), well-greased

	METRIC	IMPERIAL
Soft margarine	170 g	6 oz
Caster sugar	170 g	6 oz
3 eggs		
Vanilla essence	$\frac{1}{2}$ × 5 ml spoon	$\frac{1}{2}$ teaspoon
Milk	2 × 15 ml spoons	2 tablespoons
Self-raising flour	225 g	8 oz
Icing and decoration:		
Icing sugar	170 g	6 oz
Soft margarine	55 g	2 oz
Cocoa	1 × 15 ml spoon	1 tablespoon
Hot water	2 × 15 ml spoons	2 tablespoons

30 'Matchmaker' chocolate sticks

Dolly mixture or jellytots	55 g	2 oz
Marzipan	225 g	8 oz
Two food colourings		

Cream the margarine and sugar until really light and fluffy. Gradually beat in the eggs and the vanilla essence. Fold in the sieved flour alternately with the milk. Spoon the mixture into the pudding basin and bake in the centre of a moderately hot oven for $1\frac{1}{4}$–$1\frac{1}{2}$ hours. Leave in the bowl for 5 minutes, then turn out on to a wire tray. (I prefer a glass bowl because you can see whether the cake is sticking or not.)

Make the icing by mixing the cocoa with the hot water, then blend in the margarine and finally the sieved icing sugar. Beat to a smooth icing. Cover the cooled cake with icing. (If you wish, you can cut the cake into layers and sandwich them with the icing.)

Cut the marzipan into three roughly equal pieces. Add colouring to two of the pieces — red and green perhaps. Work some cocoa into a very small piece taken from the third left plain, and use this to make perhaps a hat and shoes. Roll out arms, legs, body and head using the two colours and the plain marzipan as you think fit. Assemble with a cocktail stick to make a Guy. The more amusing it looks, the better. Sit Guy Fawkes on top of the cake, and cover the top with the chocolate sticks to look like wood. Use the miniature sweets to represent fireworks.

Black Forest Cherry Gâteau (Schwarzwalder Kirschtorte)

This is everybody's favourite German torte. It makes a splendid centrepiece at a buffet party, and can be made the day before it is needed and kept in the refrigerator overnight. This rich Bavarian torte is made from layers of kirsch-flavoured chocolate cake (Kirschwasser is a fiery, clear cherry brandy, popular in Southern Germany) on a shortbread base and with a cherry filling. A real celebration cake, it will serve eighteen people.

Cooking time: 25–35 minutes, plus 15 minutes
Oven: 180°C, 350°F, Gas Mark 4
2 × 23 cm (9 in) sandwich tins, and large baking sheet, all greased and base-lined

	METRIC	IMPERIAL
Shortbread:		
Butter	115 g	4 oz
Caster sugar	55 g	2 oz
Plain flour	170 g	6 oz
Finely chopped walnuts	55 g	2 oz
Chocolate cake:		
4 eggs		
Caster sugar	115 g	4 oz
Self-raising flour	85 g	3 oz
Cocoa powder	30 g	1 oz
Hot water	1 × 15 ml spoon	1 tablespoon
Filling:		
Unsalted butter	170 g	6 oz
Granulated sugar	170 g	6 oz
3 egg yolks		
Plain chocolate	225 g	8 oz
Canned black cherries	450 g	15 oz
18 maraschino cherries		
Cornflour	2 × 5 ml spoons	2 teaspoons
1 wine glass of kirsch or brandy		
Double cream	275 ml	½ pint

First of all, make the shortbread. Cream the butter and sugar in a warmed bowl and then work in the walnuts and flour to make a dough. Roll it out on a floured board to a 23 cm (9 in) circle. Move this on to greased paper placed on the baking sheet. Next, make the cake. Whisk the eggs and caster sugar together until very pale, frothy and thick (like lightly-whipped cream). Gently fold in the sieved flour and cocoa with the hot water. Pour the mixture into the two prepared cake tins. Bake in the centre of a moderate oven for 25–35 minutes, or until the cakes feel springy to the touch and are *just* starting to shrink from the edges of the tin. Leave in tin for 2 minutes before turning out on to wire racks to cool. Now bake the shortbread above the centre of the oven for 15–20 minutes until pale golden brown. Leave to cool on the baking sheet.

To make the continental butter cream filling, dissolve the granulated sugar in 150 ml (¼ pint) of water over gentle heat in a small, heavy saucepan. Then bring the syrup to the boil, and boil rapidly for 5 minutes until the short thread stage is reached, or until a cooking thermometer reads 105°C (220°F). Pour the syrup on to the egg yolks, beating it in well. Continue to beat the mixture as you add the butter in small lumps. Gently melt the chocolate in a small bowl over some water in a saucepan. Add half the melted chocolate to the butter cream. Pour the rest on to a piece of greaseproof or waxed paper on a flat surface and allow it to set. When it is cold, cut into eighteen small triangles with a sharp knife. Chop up all the chocolate that's over, or grate it on to a plate, and store it in the fridge. Store the triangles in a cool place.

Drain the canned black cherries, and stone the cherries by cutting them in half (or use a cherry stoner). Blend the cornflour with the juice from the cherries and gently heat in a saucepan until the mixture comes to the boil. Cook for 2 minutes, stirring continuously until the mixture is thick and clear. Add the cherries and allow to cool. Whip the double cream with 2 × 15 ml spoons (2 tablespoons) of top of milk until thick and in peaks, but still glossy.

Now you are ready to assemble the gâteau. Place the short-bread base on your best flat serving dish — preferably one with

204

a stand. Now spread a thin layer of the chocolate butter cream on the shortbread. On the underside of the first layer of cake spread a layer of cherry mixture. Lower the first cake layer on to the shortbread. Sprinkle the top of this layer generously with half of the Kirsch or Kirschwasser — otherwise, use brandy or cherry brandy. Then put a good layer of whipped cream on to the cake and cover that with a layer of cherry mixture. On the underside of the top cake layer, spread a layer of chocolate butter cream. Lower this top layer on to the filling and sprinkle the rest of the Kirsch on to the cake.

Cover the sides of the cake with the chocolate butter cream, and press the grated chocolate over the sides of the cake. Then put some of the whipped cream into a piping bag. Use the rest of the cream over the top of the gâteau. Pipe eighteen whirls of cream around the cake and put a triangle of chocolate between each, and a drained maraschino cherry on top of each. Set aside in a very cool place or fridge for 4 hours to allow the flavours to mature.

This is a very rich gâteau, but I'll be amazed if there is anyone who doesn't enjoy it.

Initial or Number Cake

This is a simple and effective celebration cake made in the shape of the initial letter of a name, or in the shape of a number to mark a birthday or anniversary. I bake the cake in a good-sized meat roasting tray, and use a finely serrated knife to cut out the shape of the letter. The cake that is cut away can be used to make small fancy cakes, or as the basis of a trifle or for an orange fool (see the last section).

Cooking time: 50–60 minutes
Oven: 190°C, 375°F, Gas Mark 5
A meat roasting tin with a base measuring about 28 cm × 18 cm (11 in × 7 in), greased and lined

	METRIC	IMPERIAL
Soft margarine	225 g	8 oz
Caster sugar	225 g	8 oz
4 eggs		
Vanilla essence	$\frac{1}{2}$ × 5 ml spoon	$\frac{1}{2}$ teaspoon
Self-raising flour	225 g	8 oz
Icing:		
Icing sugar	450 g	1 lb
Soft margarine	170 g	6 oz
Top of milk or orange juice	6–8 × 15 ml spoons	6–8 tablespoons

Colouring and flavouring
Sugar flowers or small sweets
Candle holders and candles

In a warmed bowl, cream the soft margarine and caster sugar until light, fluffy and pale. Gradually beat in the eggs and vanilla essence with a little of the flour towards the end. Now gently fold in the sieved flour and pour into the prepared meat tray. Level off the mixture. Bake in centre of oven for 50–60 minutes until the cake is well risen, golden and springy to the touch. Leave in the tin for 4 minutes, then turn out on to a wire rack and peel off the base paper. Now take a sheet of paper — greaseproof is fine — the same size as the base of the tin, and mark out on it your letter or number. Make the largest one you can that will fit into the space. If you are making an M or a W, use the paper with the longer side as the base. If you are making the number 25, bake two cakes! Draw around the letter or number shape again, at least 6.5 cm (2½ in) away from your original line so that you have a block figure or letter. When you are satisfied with the shape and sure it will fit on to the cake, cut out the shape with scissors. You may find it easier to make your template from card — use the side of a cornflakes box. Move the cooled cake on to a wooden board or good flat surface. Gently position the template on top and secure it. if you wish. with a cocktail stick or two. Now gently and carefully remove the excess cake with a knife. making sure that you cut away to leave a vertical side to your cake all round. Trim up if necessary.

Move the cake to a serving platter and make the icing. If the cake is for an adult. a little sherry or rum could be sprinkled on to the cake at this stage (make a few holes with a cocktail stick). Sieve the icing sugar into a good-sized bowl. Mix in the soft margarine and top of milk until all is combined. Beat until the icing is very smooth and spreadable. Cover the sides of the cake first. then use the rest of the icing to cover the top. You can use some of the icing to pipe on extra decoration if you like.

Decorate with silver balls. sugar flowers or candle holders and candles.

Glacé Fruit and Nut Celebration Cake

I always decorate my own Christmas cake this way. This cake makes a marvellous present. I particularly like to give it to someone moving into a new house. The shining fruit-topped cake looks so inviting. and the fruit cake below is so sustaining. It's also rather nice to be able to offer one's new neighbours a piece of delicious cake when they call. I use the Christmas cake as a base. but you could just as well use the Dundee cake without the almonds.

These quantities will cover a 20 cm (8 in) square cake.

	METRIC	IMPERIAL
Apple jelly or sieved apricot jam	4 × 15 ml spoons	4 tablespoons
Glacé cherries (preferably red, green and yellow)	115 g	4 oz
Walnut halves	30 g	1 oz
Blanched toasted almonds	30 g	1 oz
About 6 Brazil nuts		
Some pieces of glacé pineapple if you can get it, or any other glacé fruit.		

In a small saucepan, gently heat the jelly or jam until it is runny and smooth — sieve the jam if necessary, but don't add any water. Brush the top of the cake with the warm jelly. Now arrange the fruit and nuts on top of the cake, either in diagonal lines across the cake, making sure that you contrast the colours well with each stripe, or in a random fashion. Make sure that the whole of the top of the cake is covered. Now gently spoon the rest of the jelly over the fruit and nuts to give them a very pretty shiny glaze. Secure a cake band around the cake and finish with a bow. I usually use white tissue paper for the band, folding it into three layers and making 1 cm ($\frac{1}{2}$ in) cuts close together along the top and bottom edges. I secure the overlapping ends with sticky tape and tie some gold ribbon around the cake, finishing in a bow. This cake will keep well for up to a month at least.

Bûche de Noël

A thin slice of this delicious French Christmas cake is all I can ever manage at Christmas tea. The other joy of this Christmas cake is that it freezes so well. I usually make mine about a fortnight before Christmas, but it will freeze well for a month.

Cooking time: 12–15 minutes
Oven: 200°C, 400°F, Gas Mark 6
A swiss roll tin measuring about 32 cm × 23 cm (13 in × 9 in), greased
and lined with oiled paper. Cut the paper to fit the base and ends only
— not the long sides of the tin

	METRIC	IMPERIAL
Caster sugar	100 g	3½ oz
3 eggs		
Self-raising flour	55 g	2 oz
Cocoa	30 g	1 oz
Cream filling:		
Unsalted butter	55 g	2 oz
Caster sugar	55 g	2 oz
Coffee essence	1 × 5 ml spoon	1 teaspoon
Hot water	4 × 5 ml spoons	4 teaspoons
Cold milk	5 × 5 ml spoons	5 teaspoons
Vanilla essence	¼ × 5 ml spoon	¼ teaspoon
Icing:		
Coffee essence	½ × 5 ml spoon	½ teaspoon
Cocoa	1 × 5 ml spoon	1 teaspoon
Very hot water	2 × 5 ml	2 teaspoons
Icing sugar	115 g	4 oz
Unsalted butter	55 g	2 oz
Icing sugar (decoration)	1 × 15 ml spoon	1 tablespoon

Sieve the flour and cocoa together twice and store on a plate in a
warm place. In a large warmed bowl, whisk the eggs and sugar
until thick, pale and like whipped cream. Sieve the flour and
cocoa over the egg mixture and very gently fold in. Repeat until
all has been added. Pour the mixture into the prepared tin and
bake above the centre of a hot oven for 12–15 minutes until
well risen and springy to the touch. While the cake is cooking,
spread a clean tea cloth on your working surface and sprinkle it

with caster sugar. Remove the cake from the oven, loosen the sides with a knife and turn the tin over on to the cloth. Remove the tin and peel away the paper. With a sharp knife trim away the crisp edges of the cake. Take one end of the cloth and fold it over the short end of the cake, and now continue rolling the cake with the cloth so that the cloth is taking up the space where the filling will go. This prevents the cake sticking to itself and therefore makes it easier to unroll again. Leave the cloth-covered roll on a wire rack to cool.

Now make the cream filling. Cream the butter and sugar until pale and fluffy. Using a spoonful at a time, beat in the hot water — this will dissolve the sugar. Then beat in the cold milk and the vanilla and coffee essence in the same way. Make the butter icing by mixing the coffee essence, cocoa and hot water in the bowl first of all. Then gradually mix in the sieved icing sugar and softened butter. Beat all together until smooth.

When the chocolate roll is cool, carefully unroll it on to the working surface. Spread the coffee filling over the whole cake and gently re-roll. You'll be surprised how well that works. Now move the cake on to a piece of greaseproof paper (or serving platter) and start by spreading the icing over each end of the roll. Then cover all the curved surface. Next comes the artistic bit! With a four-pronged fork, drag the prongs along the length of the roll to make the bark of a tree. Don't forget the knots — simply make the lines wavy. Make round designs at each end of the log. Now decorate with a sprig of holly and a plastic robin if you have one. Next, I take a piece of pretty Christmas ribbon and make a simple five-looped bow with it, attaching it to the cake with a large-headed pin. Finally, put the tablespoon of icing sugar into a fine sieve, and tap the edge of the sieve as you move over the log. A drift of snow will descend, making it look very effective, and good enough to eat right away. Happy Christmas!

To freeze: Carefully store the iced log in a lidded container.

To use: Allow to thaw in container overnight in a very cool place. Then decorate with the ribbon, or a message, and drift the icing sugar over the log.

Praline Cream Gâteau

This is the kind of cake you can see being lovingly carried home on Sundays from so many French Pâtisseries. It's well worth making some praline powder — a delicious mixture of caramel and roasted almonds — to keep in a lidded container on your shelves for flavouring fillings and ice cream. Instructions are given under *almonds* in the last section.

Cooking time: 25 minutes
Oven: 190°C, 375°F, Gas Mark 5
A 28 cm × 18 cm × 2.5 cm (11 in × 7 in × 1 in) baking tin, greased and base-lined

	METRIC	IMPERIAL
Caster sugar	115 g	4 oz
Soft margarine or butter	115 g	4 oz
2 eggs		
Self-raising flour	100 g	$3\frac{1}{2}$ oz
Ground almonds	30 g	1 oz
Butter cream:		
Caster sugar	115 g	4 oz
Water	1 × 15 ml spoon	1 tablespoon
2 egg yolks		
Unsalted butter	115 g	4 oz
Praline powder	55 g	2 oz
Toasted flaked almonds	30 g	1 oz
Icing:		
Icing sugar	70 g	$2\frac{1}{2}$ oz
Instant coffee	2 × 5 ml spoons	2 teaspoons

| Hot water | 2 × 5 ml spoons | 2 teaspoons |

Cream the margarine or butter and sugar until pale and fluffy.
Gradually beat in the eggs. Fold in the sieved flour and then the
ground almonds. Spread evenly into the prepared tin. Bake in
the centre of a moderate oven for 25 minutes. Leave in tin for 2
minutes, then cool on a wire rack.

Make the French butter cream by dissolving the caster sugar
with the water in a small heavy suacepan over gentle heat. Then
bring the syrup to 105°C (220°F), the point when it forms a fine
thread when pulled between finger and thumb (cool a little in a
teaspoon first). Pour the syrup on to the egg yolks in a stream,
beating all the time. As the mixture cools, gradually beat in the
butter — adding it in small pieces. Now beat in the praline
powder in two or three additions. Cut the cake in two,
lengthwise. Sandwich it with half the praline cream.

In a cup or small bowl, mix the coffee with the hot water. Add
the sieved icing sugar and beat until smooth. Pour the icing on
to the top only of the gâteau, spreading it gently with the back of
a spoon. Spread the rest of the praline cream over the sides.
Decorate by making a line of overlapping toasted split almonds
around the top and the base of the gâteau. Leave in a cold place
for 5–6 hours.

To freeze: Store the cake cut and separated by greaseproof paper in a
    lidded container or plastic bag.
To use: Thaw in container at room temperature for 1 hour — then
    decorate.

Mocha Meringue Cake

This is a wonderful last-minute celebration cake. I pile coffee meringues (see the section on small cakes) and chantilly cream really high on a glass dish with a stand, and pour mocha chocolate over the top so that it cascades down over the coffee and cream mixture in delicious streams. Irresistible!

	METRIC	IMPERIAL
24 single coffee meringues		
Double cream	225 ml	½ pint
Top of milk	4 × 15 ml spoons	4 tablespoons
Vanilla sugar	2 × 5 ml spoons	2 teaspoons
Plain chocolate	115 g	4 oz
Very strong coffee	1 × 15 ml spoon	1 tablespoon

Whisk the double cream and top of milk together, and fold in the vanilla sugar. Make a layer of nine meringues across the serving dish and cover with a layer of the sweetened cream. Now add another layer of meringues, and then the cream. Continue in this fashion, making a pyramid of the meringues with the cream — the higher the better, as long as there is no danger of a collapse! In a small bowl over hot water, gently melt the chocolate with the coffee and then spoon over the meringue structure so that the trickles look effective. Store in a very cool place for 1–2 hours to allow the meringues to soften a little, if you have time, otherwise serve at once.

GERALDENE HOLT'S CAKE STALL

STEPS TO SUCCESS

I hope this section will help you to get really good results with your own cakes and biscuits. The comforting aroma of a freshly-baked cake is a great encouragement to all home bakers, and in over twenty years of home baking I have learnt that there are two golden rules for success.

First, enjoy what you are doing — don't worry too much if little things don't quite work out. Remind yourself that all of us are improving all the time. And secondly — find out what you are doing, and why: that way you will gain an understanding of the art, and see how to make those improvements.

To help with both these aims, I am jotting down some information which I hope will be of help not only to novices, but also to those who have been baking for several years but are just a bit hazy about some of the background details.

Kitchen Equipment and Techniques

WEIGHING

I know that many good cooks guess the weights of their ingredients, but I find that usually they cook only a narrow range of dishes. To repeat culinary successes and try new recipes, you really need to measure quantities correctly. If you are starting out to cook now, it's a good idea to use the metric system. But I know that older people will always prefer the imperial system, and so I have written and tested all the recipes in both systems, and worked out what I think is the best equivalence between the two. After all, the cake you make should be the same size, whichever way you weigh. I have tried both spring and balance-type scales, and find the old balance type both more dependable, and usable with either system of weighing. If you would like to convert yourself to metric from imperial, all you need do with balance scales is fix yourself up with a set of metric weights. This comprises: 1 kg, 500 g, 200 g (twice), 100 g, 50 g, 20 g (twice), 10 g, and 5 g. With these ten weights you can weigh out all you need. You will find a conversion table and other useful information at the beginning of this book.

BASIC EQUIPMENT

Here is a list of the basic equipment which you will need to be able to get off the ground. Even so, there is always room for improvisation — a great many cakes can be mixed in a saucepan. So you can start in a small way and gradually acquire extra items from the list.

Mixing bowls: it helps to have bowls of three different sizes. The largest should be about 30 cm (12 in) across the top — I call this a good-sized bowl.

Sieve: use a sieve of nylon or metal mesh. This is essential for sieving flour and icing sugar.

Measuring jug: I prefer a clear heatproof glass jug with both metric and imperial measures marked on the side.

Flexible spatula: a plastic or rubber spatula is ideal for scraping mixture from bowls.

Palette knife: the standard 18 cm (7 in) blade one is invaluable. I also find a smaller one with a 13 cm (5 in) blade very useful.

Measuring spoons: it helps to have a set of plastic spoons giving 1 tablespoon, 1 teaspoon, $\frac{1}{2}$ teaspoon and $\frac{1}{4}$ teaspoon.

Wooden spoon: you can't have too many of these. Even the handles come in useful for making brandy snaps.

Kitchen timer: some timing device is essential. I use the timer on my cooker, but the portable ones are useful too. Otherwise keep your eye on a clock or watch, and jot down when a cake goes in the oven, and when it should come out.

Whisk: a wire balloon whisk is excellent but rather long-winded. A hand-turned beater is much quicker, and an electric hand-held beater faster still — this is a most useful piece of kitchen equipment. See also electric mixer, below.

Baking tins: at the risk of turning you into a hoarder, like me, I'd say you can't have too many. (You can always grow mustard and cress in those you don't use!) Beg or buy at least a round tin, a loaf tin, a good-sized baking sheet or swiss roll tin, a rectangular tray about 28 cm by 18 cm (11 in by 7 in), and some patty tins — I prefer the non-stick variety but I still grease and line them: then they are easier to keep clean. To this list I would urge you to add, in time, two 18 cm (7 in) sandwich tins, a ring cake tin, and a 20 cm (8 in) spring form tin, a flan tin, madeleine tins and a griddle. And if you double up on your original tins you can bake more cakes at the same time. Most department stores and hardware shops have good displays of baking tins, and so do some of the grocery chains. Often excellent tins come up at jumble sales and market stalls: all they need is a good scrub with wire wool. I usually bring tins and other kitchen equipment back with me from holidays abroad. I also collect any clean smooth tins for baking different-shaped cakes in — like the tins for malt extract that come with beer kits. Providing they are a simple shape, and well greased and lined they work very well. N.B. A $\frac{1}{2}$ kg (1 lb) loaf tin holds about 840 ml ($1\frac{1}{2}$ pints).

Plastic or wooden ruler: you need this for checking the size of cake tins, and when using marzipan.

Rolling-pin: I prefer a wooden one of simple design, not too short.

Pastry board: this is not essential, if you have a laminate work-top — but I prefer to work on wood. Even a smooth piece of blockboard would do.

Pastry brush: use either a plastic one with nylon bristles, sold for the job, or a clean 2.5 cm (1 in) paint brush.

Shaped cutters: these can be bought, fluted or plain, often in sets and sometimes in their own tin. Eventually add a set for making petits fours, a gingerbread man and other special shapes like animals, teddy bears and so on.

Wire rack: this is an essential item, so that cakes can cool with air circulating around them.

Icing set: instead of the metal cylinder icing tube, I prefer a nylon piping bag which can be fitted with three or four different nozzles. It is useful also for making éclairs, meringues, and for piping whipped cream.

Large spoon, knife and fork, and teaspoon: try to find some old cutlery that can be kept specially for baking.

Greaseproof paper: you need this for lining cake tins. and for resting cakes on while icing them.

Non-stick paper: this invention is a great boon: 'Bakewell' seems a good make. It's invaluable if your meringues stick.

Oven glove, cloth and apron: I think this basic protective clothing is essential. And if you bake with bare arms, you may need to add cloth to your gloves to protect them when you have to reach into the back of the oven. Never lift a hot tin from the oven with a damp cloth — a dry cloth insulates much better.

Plates for serving: I collect flat plates or wooden platters for serving cakes — the ordinary dished dinner plate is not much good. On the Continent special flat glass or porcelain serving plates are sold. They support the cake properly and look much nicer. Keep your eye open for pretty old plates in junk shops, jumble sales or on market stalls. You can use round wooden bread boards for serving scones and tea-breads, and meringues and special cakes look super on cake stands. There are still lots of Victorian glass ones around, or you can try Habitat for modern white china versions.

Grater: use a round or square stainless-steel grater with different teeth for cheese, nutmeg, orange rind and so on.

Lemon squeezer: a glass or plastic one is useful.

Notebook and pencil: you need it to jot down your own ideas, as well as cooking times and ingredients to buy.

Electric mixer: there's a clear-cut case for buying an electric mixer if you do a lot of baking or have a big family — although some people argue for the therapeutic value of beating and mixing by hand. If you would like a mixer and enjoy baking, read on to the end of the book and see how you can afford one!

Ingredients

I am often asked about the use of the various common ingredients used in home bakery. So here are a few notes about the materials which are most often used.

Plain flour is the flour most widely used — in America it is known as all-purpose flour. It is a soft flour, excellent for pastry, biscuits and cakes. In some recipes it is used with a raising agent, like baking powder. If in any doubt which flour to use, stick to plain flour. Self-raising flour is a relatively modern introduction, and in old recipes plain flour is always intended. 1 heaped tablespoon weighs approximately 30 g (1 oz).

Self-raising flour (in America, self-rising) is plain soft flour to which a raising agent has been added in the right proportion for most cakes. Sometimes all-in-one-mix or quick-mix cakes use self-raising flour plus baking powder. 1 heaped tablespoon weighs approximately 30 g (1 oz).

Wholewheat flour is the flour from which plain flour is made by further milling and sifting; so wholewheat flour contains the total goodness of the grain. As well as trace elements, vitamins and small amounts of minerals, it contains the fibre which is essential for proper digestion. Don't try to sieve wholewheat flour — you will simply separate out the fibre. If you have difficulty buying wholewheat (or wholemeal) flour, try health food shops. They usually sell it in both plain and self-raising packs.

Cornflour, or cornstarch, is a highly refined flour starch made from Indian corn or maize. It gives a soft texture to cakes, and is used in some biscuits.

Rice flour, or ground rice, is a more granular form of starch. It is often used in biscuits, and in some recipes as a partial replacement for ground almonds.

Butter: the unsalted sort is usually Dutch, French or German, and is the most widely used fat in French baking. It imparts a delicate flavour and moistness to biscuits and cakes. It is excellent in all home baking, but expensive. Salted butter is usually a darker colour. It may be English, Welsh or Irish, or can often be a blend of butters from various sources.

Margarine is a whipped vegetable fat or oil mixed with skimmed milk, flavouring and Vitamins A and D. It can be bought in saturated or polyunsaturated forms. Soft margarine is a pale, very soft form. Block or hard margarine is darker and sometimes contains more salt.

Soft margarine is ideal for making cakes, biscuits and pastry. Best used at room temperature, it speeds up mixing and can go straight into all-in-one mixes. It is an excellent and economical substitute for butter in baking — I find that very few people use butter for baking these days. You can also use half butter and half margarine as a replacement.

Lard is whitish animal fat which I never buy or use: I think it has a leadening effect on cakes and pastry. But it was much used in the past, before the introduction of margarine or vegetable fat.

Vegetable fat is known as shortening in America, and is a light, white whipped fat excellent in pastry mixed with half margarine or butter. Some recipes (mainly American) use vegetable fat in cakes and pastries. At room temperature it creams or rubs in very easily..

Vegetable oil: the best oil to use in baking is corn oil, made from maize: it has only a *mild* flavour. Cake mixtures using oil are easy to prepare and have a batter-like consistency. Oil-based cakes have a slightly heavier, crumbly texture, and extra raising agent is usually necessary to counteract this.

Granulated sugar is the cheapest white sugar, and the coarsest. It is generally used for cooking fruit, etc. It crops up in some cake recipes, usually of the rubbed-in type.

Caster sugar (confectioner's sugar in America) is the white sugar normally used in baking. It creams with butter much more effectively than granulated sugar. You can make your own caster sugar by grinding granulated sugar in a liquidiser for $\frac{1}{2}$ minute.

Icing sugar is a very fine white sugar used in royal icing, glacé icing and other English icings and fillings. Keep it dry, and always sieve it before using.

Demerara sugar is the coarsest sugar, less refined than white sugar. It is pale brown in colour and, compared with white sugar, has a honeyed flavour.

Light soft brown sugar is a fine, beige sugar with a delicate caramel flavour.

Dark soft brown sugar, or Barbados sugar, is a dark brown moist sugar, little refined and with a toffee flavour. It is useful in fruit cakes.

For most sugars, 1 rounded tablespoon is approximately 30 g (1 oz).

Golden syrup is a very sweet golden liquid sugar which helps to keep cakes moist. One level tablespoon weighs about 30 g (1 oz).

Treacle, or molasses, is a dark, almost black syrup made in the course of refining sugar. It is not as sweet as golden syrup, and has a strong caramel flavour. It is used in rich fruit cakes. One level tablespoon weighs roughly 30 g (1 oz).

Honey is a naturally produced form of sugar, which helps to keep cakes moist, and gives an attractive sheen when brushed over the top of warm cakes. Set honey can be turned into clear, runny honey by keeping the jar in a warm place (like an airing cupboard) for 2–3 days. One level tablespoon weighs about 30 g (1 oz).

Eggs: these are the main raising agent in baking. Absolutely new-laid eggs are not as good for baking as those that are 3 or 4 days old and have lost just a little moisture — the new-laid are better boiled for breakfast. Keep eggs at a cool temperature: at the bottom of your fridge if your kitchen is very hot, but take them out and let them reach room temperature before using them. They will then mix much better, and the yolks will separate more easily from the whites. You can buy plastic egg separator gadgets.

It is always a good idea, when using eggs, to crack each egg into a cup or saucer before adding it to the mix. You can check that the egg is sound, and prevent any shell getting in too.

The most commonly used egg size is Size 3. This weighs about 55 g (2 oz) and is equivalent to the old standard egg. My recipes assume this size, but most will work with Size 2, which is a bit larger.

Another good idea, especially when batch baking, is to crack the eggs needed into a glass measuring jug and check that you are using the same total volume of eggs each time. This is a help if you are using a variety of egg sizes, or cracked eggs. You might make a note in your cookbook of the number of fluid ounces of egg you use.

Baking powder: cooks used to make up their own baking powder. Alison Uttley describes this in her *Recipes from an Old Farmhouse.* Today we buy commercial baking powder, which

224

is a mixture of bicarbonate of soda and cream of tartar. When mixed with liquid, it effervesces and releases carbon dioxide. This means that if you have made a mixture containing a raising agent other than eggs, the mix should go into the oven as soon as possible or the raising effect will be reduced.

Bicarbonate of soda, or baking soda, is a raising agent with a more gentle action then baking powder. It has a stronger effect when mixed with cream of tartar.

Cream of tartar is a fast-acting raising agent which begins to react at room temperature, as soon as it is in contact with the liquid.

Fruit: the most commonly used fruit in baking is dried fruit, although some of the nicest fruit cakes do make use of fresh fruit (see Fruit Cakes). Today, dried fruit has been washed and dried before sale: but I can remember my mother washing her fruit free from bits of stalk and drying it in the sun.

Four main kinds of grapes are used for dried fruit, giving us:
(1) seeded raisins — these are big, flat, sticky raisins with a muscatel flavour, which usually need cutting before adding to Christmas puddings or fruit cakes. They are delicious eaten alone or with nuts;
(2) seedless raisins — made from smaller black grapes which look brown when dried. They don't need cutting, but still have a honey and muscatel flavour;
(3) sultanas — made from white grapes, and which look yellow when dried. They give a marvellous moisture to any cake; and
(4) currants — these are dried small black grapes, with a sweet, nutty flavour. They are usually used with sultanas or raisins but you find them on their own in cookies or biscuits.

You may find it more convenient or economical to buy packets of mixed dried fruit, which will contain seedless raisins, sultanas and currants and some chopped candied peel. This mixture is fine for a wide range of fruit cakes, or in fruit scones and buns. When using dried fruit in rich fruit cakes, it is a good idea to soak the fruit overnight in the liquid from the recipe — in orange juice, sherry or whatever. Then it will plump up. Other dried fruits, like figs, dates and apricots are very useful in baking and give us the variety we need.

Candied peel is the outer skin of citrus fruit — orange, lemon, grapefruit and citron — which has been preserved by soaking in syrup and kept in sugar. Candied peel is sold chopped, but the best is sold by the piece. It is expensive, so I often make my own.

HOME-MADE CANDIED PEEL

Cut two oranges, lemons or grapefruit each into quarters. Using a spoon or knife, gently peel off the skin. Remove as much pith as possible. Soak the peel in 600 ml (1 pint) of water mixed with $\frac{1}{2} \times 5$ ml spoon ($\frac{1}{2}$ teaspoon) of bicarbonate of soda for 30 minutes. Rinse in clean water and drain. Now cover the peel with cold water and simmer for 30–45 minutes, until tender. Retain 275 ml ($\frac{1}{2}$ pint) of the liquor, pour away the rest and drain the peel. Put the 275 ml ($\frac{1}{2}$ pint) back into the saucepan. Add 225 g (8 oz) of granulated sugar and dissolve over low heat. Now boil the syrup and bring up to 115°C (238°F) or until a little syrup dropped into cold water forms a soft ball. Add the peel and simmer for 10 minutes. Remove the peel and drain. Roll the peel in granulated sugar and store in a lidded container.

If the peel hardens in storage simply soften in boiling water, drain well and use it.

Glacé cherries are candied red cherries, also available coloured green and yellow. If they are too syrupy, wash and dry them before using. They improve any fruit cake.

Angelica is the stem of the angelica plant, preserved in sugar syrup. It is valuable for its green colour and subtle flavour.

Nuts should be kept in airtight containers to conserve their flavour: preferably away from light and in a refrigerator. Some people keep them in the freezer. Stale (but not rancid) nuts can be freshened by heating on a dish in a very hot oven for a few minutes.

Peanuts are the cheapest nuts. They are not as widely used here as in America. Although they have a strong taste (especially if roasted and salted), I find they are very useful chopped in biscuits and cookies.

Walnuts have a more gentle flavour. It's much cheaper to buy broken walnuts and, if they are to be chopped, more sensible.

Coconut is used desiccated in cooking. I buy the unsweetened kind. Toasted under the grill, it is useful for decorating the sides of a cake.

Hazelnuts, particularly when roasted, impart a subtle, sweet taste in baking. They are especially good when ground and incorporated into a meringue mixture and sandwiched with cream.

Almonds are the most useful nuts of all. Bought raw without their shells but still in their brown skins, you can blanch them simply by pouring boiling water over them, leaving for 5 minutes, pouring off the water and squeezing off the skins. They are also sold ready-blanched, split or halved, chopped (nibbed) and flaked. The best way of using almonds as a flavouring in cream, ice cream and icing is as praline, which is a mixture of toasted almonds and caramelised sugar. It keeps well as a powder in an airtight container.

Roast 115 g (4 oz) of blanched split almonds in the oven or under the grill until they are golden brown. Dissolve 115 g (4 oz) of granulated sugar in 2 × 15 ml spoons (2 tablespoons) of water in a small heavy saucepan over gentle heat. Once the sugar is dissolved, add the almonds and increase the heat so that the sugar caramelises. When it is a golden orange brown, pour carefully into a buttered tin or on to buttered greaseproof paper. When it has set, cover with a sheet of paper and crush by flattening it with a rolling pin until a fine powder results. Store in a lidded jar.

The most common use for almonds in cooking is as ground almonds. Because one-half their weight is oil, ground almonds keep cakes moist and give them a distinctive flavour. They are also the main ingredients in almond paste, or marzipan.

Other nuts used in baking are pecan, cashews and brazil nuts. If you have difficulty buying nuts, try health food stores.

Chocolate: true dark baker's chocolate is getting difficult to obtain. Good quality plain chocolate works just as well. Coating chocolate is useful for decorating cookies, etc, but don't use it instead of cooking chocolate — it has a very high palm oil content which allows it to melt at a low temperature, but which reacts unfavourably with liquid. The plain coating chocolate is superior to the milk chocolate version.

Spices should be bought in small quantities (unless you are starting a gingerbread factory), and kept away from the light in covered containers to retain their full aroma. Spices are one of the most valuable ingredients used in baking: for a good account of them, see Elizabeth David's *Spices, Salt and Aromatics in the English Kitchen*. A basic list for use in baking would include: allspice, aniseed, caraway seeds, cardamom seeds, cinnamon, cloves (whole and ground), ginger (stem and ground), mace, nutmeg (wholenut grated for the best flavour, as you need it) and mixed spice.

Flavourings and essences: the main essences or extracts used in baking are almond, peppermint and vanilla. But many others can be used, some of which seem rather artificial. It's always better to use real orange juice, sherry or rum rather than rely on chemical replacements. Make your own vanilla sugar by keeping a vanilla pod in a jar of caster sugar. As you use the sugar in recipes or for sprinkling on cakes, top the jar up. If you have vanilla sugar, use it in place of caster sugar and vanilla essence in any recipe.

When using colouring agents, always add them drop by drop from the end of a skewer.

Try combining a familiar flavour with another — cinnamon, for example, with chocolate, or vanilla and coffee. The combination gives a surprising degree of extra depth to the flavour.

Making the Most of Your Time

All of us are busy, and some people tell me they are too busy to make cakes. This is a pity, because a great many cakes and biscuits take very little time to make, and the results are well worth it. And the process itself is so enjoyable — but then, I'm the sort of person who would rather spend an evening in the kitchen with some nice recipes, listening to the radio, than slumped in front of the TV set.

The first essential when starting to bake is to have a plan. I always try very hard not to have to put just one cake in the oven. Write down how much time you have available — 1 hour, 2 hours, all day — in which to do your baking. Then decide what you would really like to make (this is a very enjoyable moment!), write down the temperature and the cooking time, and see if you can find the recipe of another cake you can bake at the same time. You may decide to do some *batch baking* — instead of just one chocolate cake, you can bake four and store three in the freezer. Or you may decide to bake a succession of different cakes or cookies, so that you can lay in a stock for the holidays. Or you may be running a cake stall for charity, or for yourself. By doing this you will save not only time, but heat. Remember, though, that when you bake four cakes at once in the oven, they will take just a little longer than when baking only one — but it is usually only a matter of a few minutes. Above all, batch baking requires organisation if you are to make the most of the time and heat available. If you are batch baking to sell, you must be consistent in your baking. Each cake of the same type should always be the same size and weight. This is not as difficult as it sounds. Just keep to the recipe, weigh everything carefully, and check that when you are making, for instance, $\frac{1}{2}$ kg (1 lb) loaf cakes in identical tins, the tin plus the mixture weighs the same for each one. I simply put the tin on the scales and add the mixture until it weighs the correct amount — write this figure, of course, in your notebook. Then all the cakes are repeatable. When making three or four times the amount given in the recipe, note the new quantities in a column beside the recipe — making clear by how much you've enlarged the recipe.

I always start a baking session with the cakes that need the highest temperature, like scones, then come down to sponge cakes and tea-breads, and end up with fruit cakes or meringues which need both a lower temperature and a longer time. Nothing is more bothersome than having a traffic queue of cakes waiting to go in the oven, but held up because one started the day baking something that needed a long time to cook.

I often begin a baking day by making four sheets of biscuits or cookies. Then I turn the oven on. In this way you can slip the biscuits into the oven either at the start, or in gaps between the other items. The ideal way of keeping the gaps filled, and ensuring that the oven is never empty when it's on, is to keep a roll of refrigerator cookie dough by you — this will keep splendidly in the fridge for at least a week and can be sliced, placed on a greased baking sheet and slipped into the oven before you can say Eliza Acton.

Keep not only a cookie mixture made up: save time by making up batches of dry pastry mixes or scone mixtures to which only the liquid need be added. These dry mixes will keep perfectly well in a fridge for 10–14 days and, of course, for up to 3 months in a freezer. Keep them in plastic bags or lidded boxes — old ice cream cartons or 4 lb soft margarine containers are excellent for this.

Don't forget, too, that using a kitchen timer is an important way of economising on time and heat. It not only prevents waste: it ensures consistent results, and means you can repeat your successes with no element of luck. Another useful time-saving idea is to use a pencil or felt-tip pen to mark a scale in inches or centimetres along the top edge of a drawer, or perhaps down the side of a cupboard door. Then you can measure the size of a cake tin in a trice by holding it against the scale.

If you cook on a solid fuel or oil-fired cooker like an Aga or Rayburn, a kettle of water at the back of the stove or beside the hotplate will keep at a very useful temperature. In any event, never waste hot boiled water — I always pour any I have over from making tea or coffee into a vacuum flask. This is then invaluable for warming the mixing bowl or for mixing with cocoa, or into icing.

When batch baking cakes that are to be sandwiched, I save oven space by using one deeper tin in place of two shallow ones. Then it is simply a matter of cutting the one cake into two layers before filling it, instead of sandwiching two separately-baked cakes.

To cut lining paper for the bases of cake tins, fold sheets of greaseproof paper so that they are just a little bigger than the base of the tin. Then draw round the base of the tin with a pencil, and cut through all the sheets of paper. I usually produce at least a dozen at once this way, and stockpile the circles. They are a great help on a busy day. I find that a quick way of greasing lining paper is to grease the cake tin sides, and very generously grease the base. Then smooth the base lining paper into the bottom of the tin, lift it up gently, turn it over and smooth down again.

When weighing a sticky ingredient, like syrup, or a messy one, like cocoa, it's often quicker to put the container on the scales, note the weight, and remove the ingredients from the container until the scales have fallen by the required amount. An alternative method, which I always use when weighing sugar and fat, is to make a bed of the weighed sugar in the scale pan on which to weigh the margarine or butter before tipping both into the mixing bowl. This way you keep the scale pan clean and save on washing up. This is a good dodge, too, when weighing syrup or treacle with sugar. Otherwise you can weigh the dry ingredients on pieces of greaseproof paper.

I try never to throw anything away — odd bits of cake mixture can be cooked in a heatproof pudding dish or ramekin and used in a pudding. Keep any icing you have over — it will often make a sauce for ice cream, or it can be used as a sweetener when making ice cream, or a cheese cake. If suitable, left-over icing can sweeten fruit — for example, orange glacé icing can be used when stewing rhubarb.

I get rather shocked to hear of people throwing ingredients away. A bachelor I know threw some egg whites away because he didn't know what to do with them. It's a good idea to jot down, at the back of your recipe book, the names of the recipes which use just egg whites or egg yolks (I devised Fairy Rings for this reason), or no butter or no eggs, and so on. It's worth remembering that 2 egg yolks can often be used to replace 1 whole egg in a recipe, especially where the mixture is not expected to rise a great deal — for instance, in most biscuit and cookie recipes. I usually use my extra egg yolks to make a real egg custard.

EGG CUSTARD

Simply cook 2 egg yolks, 275 ml ($\frac{1}{2}$ pint) of creamy milk and 1 × 5 ml spoon (1 teaspoon) of cornflour with 2 × 5 ml spoon (2 teaspoons) of vanilla sugar in a double boiler, very gently, until the custard coats the back of the spoon.

You can serve the custard hot or cold — it's particularly good on a really boozy trifle. Once you've tasted an egg custard, you'll never buy custard powder again. Any egg or part of an egg can, of course, be used in scrambled eggs.

Just occasionally you may have a slight baking mishap: you

may drop a cake or singe one side, or find — if you are running a cake stall — that an odd sponge cake has been left unsold. Such cakes are excellent for use in a trifle, or for making a delicious orange fool.

ORANGE FOOL

Break the sponge cake into small pieces and arrange in an attractive glass bowl. Grate the rind from 4 oranges and 2 lemons into another bowl, add the juice from the fruit and stir in caster sugar to taste. Pour 570 ml (1 pint) of single cream into the fruit juice, stir and pour over the cake. Put in a very cold place to mellow for at least 6 hours, or overnight.

Selling Cakes

I started to sell cakes by selling other people's cakes — on cake stalls at church bazaars, school fêtes and other fund-raising events. You've seen how quickly the home-made cake stall sells out at these functions — it meant I had time to browse round the bargains at the other stalls! So when I started my own cake stall at a Friday morning market, I felt sure that as long as I produced good, home-baked cakes and biscuits at the right price they would sell. In fact, I discovered I could hardly keep up with the demand. I'm convinced that if every local market had a home-baking stall, demand would still not be satisfied — there is unlimited scope. In some parts of the country, of course, the Women's Institute run a stall selling home-baked cakes along with eggs, vegetables and so on. They have produced a helpful booklet on market trading. So if you like baking and would prefer to work from home, I would encourage you to go ahead. Most people have a market within 10 miles of them, and often much nearer than that. First, though, read the rest of this section: because once you enter the world of food merchandising, you must know how certain laws and statutes affect you.

An important point is that, under the provisions of the Food and Drugs Act 1955, the premises on which food is prepared must be open to inspection by the local environmental health officer. In my experience these are friendly and helpful, and a quick phone call to ask his (or her) advice at the outset of your venture is very wise. He may decide to call on you just to check that you have a kitchen and food store in a hygienic state, and that you have access to proper toilet and washing facilities. (These regulations were framed for the catering industry, but they still apply.)

As in any production business, maximum profit will be assured if the costs are kept to a minimum; so I would advise you to purchase your raw materials as cheaply as possible. This does not mean lowering the standard of the product — indeed, you may end up still using your local branch of multiple grocers. I often find I can buy the cheapest and best flour in one of these, if not from the local mill. But it probably does mean bulk buying for some ingredients, although by no means all of them. And at the start, one doesn't want to tie up too much money in storage.

A visit, therefore, to your local cash and carry food market may be a good idea. I have found the kind intended for shop and restaurant owners the most advantageous. Ask to see the manager and explain what you are up to; then a customer's card allows you to buy your bulk baking materials there. I find the biggest savings are made on dried fruit, cocoa, nuts and wrapping materials.

When I started my cake stall I used all my own hens' eggs, but I soon found they couldn't turn them out fast enough. I discovered a nearby egg farmer who would sell me trays of eggs at a good price. I also learnt about cracked eggs: these are eggs with hairline cracks in the shell, but for which the farmer gets very little from the egg packing stations. So they are often sold off to commercial bakeries, or to people like me. You usually have to collect them yourself. One good way of storing cracked eggs is to break them into lidded jam jars or plastic containers, eight at a time, and keep them in the fridge. Write on the lid how many eggs, whites or yolks the jar contains. Remember, though, to take them out in good time for baking, so that they come up to room temperature.

Once you feel that you've got your sources of supply worked out, you'll have to decide how to sell your produce. I think these are the main ways of selling home-produced fare:

1 to friends;
2 to shops and restaurants;
3 from your house;

4 using a delivery service;
5 from a van;
6 in a market.

Each of these methods has its own advantages. You must decide which is the best for you when you have taken all your circumstances into account. I think selling to friends could operate well if you have only a limited amount of time, but love cooking. I know that a great many busy mums jump at the chance of buying wholesome, tasty cakes and biscuits for their family. Not everyone enjoys baking, and your customers might then have more time to follow their own pursuit. This could be to their advantage, and yours — a system of simple barter might result, and everyone's lot be improved. Women, in particular, can suffer much stress from trying to be good at everything — and over half the married women in this country have jobs.

You may live in an area where selling to shops and restaurants is preferable. But be careful here, because once you are not selling direct to your customers you may find your profit margin diminished. I find, too, that the satisfaction one gets from selling direct is an advantage — I have made many new friends on my cake stall. You may be able to sell directly from your house, but you must check the legal position here. You may be turning your house into a shop from the point of view of the planning acts. One way round this may be to deliver your cakes. Some small advertisements in your local paper telling your customers of your wares — be they cakes, biscuits, pizzas or pies — should keep your phone ringing with orders from those who are planning parties, or simply wanting to stock up their freezer. Selling straight from a van is doubtless possible, but perhaps risky until you've built up a regular round as a basis. But I'd love to see lots of vans going around saying 'Penelope's Pride' and 'Susan's Pride' on their sides, rather than 'Mother's'. Selling in a market or from a van must comply with the Food Hygiene Act 1966 (Amended), available from HMSO.

I found that the local market had many advantages. First of all, the selling goes on for only one day a week (although I was mad enough to go twice a week at one stage). This means you have plenty of time to make your fare in the four to five days before the market. I start by baking fruit cakes and biscuits, because these keep well. Gingerbread only improves with 3 days' keeping, leading up to scones and sponges which are sold as freshly as possible. You soon become established at the same stall in a weekly market. You'll be amazed how quickly regular customers build up, which means that your order book begins to bulge and you reduce the risk element. On the subject of risks it is wise to take out insurance to cover yourself against unexpected mishaps. Another point in favour of the market is that the overheads are low. The hire of a stall varies from place to place, and it is more expensive in London than down here in Devon — but then, the selling price of your produce will reflect this. Don't work for next to nothing — you must reckon to pay yourself a fair and reasonable rate, taking into account that you are working in your own home, at your own convenience. You are on a flexible time system, without the expense of travelling to work. As a guide to prices, note the prices of the highest class of commercially-produced cakes and charge at least that. Your produce should be superior in every way.

Every market has a supervisor, normally employed by the local authority, to whom you must apply for a stall. In some areas there are waiting lists. But I have found that a great many markets are low on stall-holders and are in need of a surge of interest to revive them. It is, of course, one of the earliest forms of trading, and one of the most satisfying. My cake stall is in a pannier market, the name indicating how traders arrived with their panniers laden — as do I — to return home with coins jingling in their pockets! And while on the subject of money, it is essential to keep a careful and detailed record of expenditure and income, so that you know where you are. You might, after all, end up in the super-tax bracket.

There are certain regulations governing the sale of cooked food in markets, and these may be subject to local variation. It is necessary to have your name and address boldly displayed: this doesn't stop you, though, from giving your stall a name as well, like 'Sarah's Scones' or 'The Home Health Bakery'. I find Letraset is an effective way of making a sign on to cartridge paper or coloured ticket board. Wrap the sign carefully when you transport it. Next, all the fare sold must be covered: and this brings me to the subject of presentation. How you present yourself and your product will quite definitely affect your sales figures, whatever the quality of your product.

I made a cloth and matching aprons in a pretty Liberty print in pink and white. There is plenty of scope here for imaginative thinking. I used white cake boxes tied with pink string, and carried the colour scheme through to the pink and white ging-ham labels and covers for the home-made jam. I can imagine, for instance, a stall selling simply a whole range of scones and the home-made jam to put on them: this would look good on a hessian cloth, with inviting oatmeal colours to complement it.

I pack biscuits in small plastic bags, sealed with twist-ties and priced with self-adhesive descriptive labels. You can wrap cakes in plastic cling film — a big roll of this goes a long way — or put them on paper plates and cover them with cellophane using sellotape to secure it. The grander cakes look best in proper cake boxes. Use the Yellow Pages to find a local cheap source of these items — paper bags and wrapping tissue usually come cheapest from the same place. This packaging not only means you comply with the law — it also greatly facilitates the task of transporting the cakes. I pack the cakes and biscuits into card-board boxes, or into empty wooden tomato boxes. These stack easily and are convenient to carry. But you might be lucky and light on some metal racks or proper bakers' trays.

At Christmas I use red, green and white as the dominant colours, and decorate the stall with a small Christmas tree laden with cookies. Presentation boxes of home-baked biscuits make lovely presents, and I find that attractively wrapped Dundee cakes are snapped up as gifts. I like to reflect the seasons and festivals in my baking — variety is an essential element in life.

I hope I have given you some idea of what it is like to run a cake stall, and perhaps I have encouraged you to do the same. But whatever your interest in home baking — even if your activities have so far been confined to consuming it — I hope this book has been of value to you. I still wonder why baking is such a satisfying activity. I suppose it is because it is an act of creation. But whatever the whys and wherefores, I hope this book will help you with the hows. Good cooking!